The Women's Press Ltd
34 Great Sutton Street, London EC1V 0DX

114

Anne Finger is the author of a collection of short stories, *Basic Skills* (University of Missouri, 1988). Her fiction and non-fiction have appeared in many publications, including *Thirteenth Moon, Feminist Studies, Socialist Review*, the *San Francisco Chronicle*, and the anthology *Test-Tube Women*. She is the recipient of numerous awards including the *Southern Review*/Louisiana State University Short Fiction Award, 1988; Literature Fellowship, Brody Arts Fund, 1988; and the Associated Writing Programs Award for Short Fiction, 1987.

Acknowledgments

This book could not have been written without child care provided by Gloria Miranda, Anya Rudnick and the staff of both PICSI Center and A Children's Place in Santa Monica.

Holly Prado, Barbara Crane, Josie Martin, Betty Greenberg, Linda Berg, Rae Wilken, Celia Woloch, Toke Hoppenbroewers, Marla Petal, Barbara Waxman, Frank Clancy, Michelle Hensley, Janet Gallagher, Robin Siegal and Nina Kleinberg all read early drafts of this and provided helpful comments and advice.

Tandy Parks, Laura Graas, Lisa Manning, Susan Finger and so many others that I don't have space to name them all provided love and support during the difficult year after my child's birth and thus made this book possible. Special thanks are due to my mother, Mary El Finger, and sister, Jane Finger.

Thanks to William MacDuff for assistance with preparation of the manuscript.

Much thanks to the Barbara Deming Memorial Fund whose timely help and encouragement made the completion of this book possible.

My editor, Faith Conlon, provided insightful help and suggestions during the revising of this book. Her steadiness and enthusiasm have been a great help to me.

This book could not have been written without the insights and challenges of the women's movement and the disability rights movement.

PAST DUE

A STORY OF DISABILITY, PREGNANCY AND BIRTH

Anne Finger

The Women's Press

For Mark and Max

First published in Britain by The Women's Press Ltd 1991
A member of the Namara Group
34 Great Sutton Street
London EC1V 0DX

First published in the USA by
Seal Press in 1990

Portions of this book appeared, in slightly different form, as
the story 'Abortion', first published in *Feminist Studies*,
Summer 1985 (reprinted in the book *Basic Skills*, University
of Missouri Press, 1988), and the story 'Aftereffects', first
published in *Kaleidoscope*, January 1989.

Printed and bound in Britain by
BPCC Hazell Books
Aylesbury, Bucks
A member of BPCC Ltd

ONE

1

I was working in an abortion clinic when I found out I was pregnant.

I'd woken up at four that morning. I'd had all-you-can-eat sushi the night before and had drunk glass after glass of water to wash down the salty fish and the hot green wasabi. I staggered down the stairs in the dark and found an old jam jar in the cabinet under the sink, and peed and peed and peed. I screwed the lid on tight, a piece of plastic between the jar and the lid so that the urine wouldn't leak into my backpack.

I got to work at the Feminist Women's Health Center a little after seven. As I walked up to the building with some of my co-workers, Heidi started calling to us: "Jesus loves you. Jesus loves your baby." We know her name because she has picketed the clinic for years. She followed us all the way around the clinic, then realized that we were not there for abortions.

"You will have to answer to God for killing babies." She had dyed blonde hair in a fifties Connie Stevens-style bouffant. "Please," she called to us, "Jesus doesn't want you to kill babies."

We walked through the door and she tried again: "Nothing's been added to you but nutrition since the moment you were conceived."

At the clinic, I leaned my cane in the corner and slid off my backpack.

"*Early* morning urine," I said to Arla, one of my co-workers. (The early pregnancy test only works on the first, most concentrated, urine of the day.) "Shall I put it in the fridge?"

She nodded her head. "I'm going to run the tests about noon." I was already pretty sure I was pregnant. My period was due that day, and I'd had none of my usual premenstrual feelings. About ten days before, I'd been riding the Muni in San Francisco when a boy sat down next to me and began to eat peanuts and the smell made me nauseous.

But still, I took the test the day my period was due. I suppose that just goes to prove that no matter how much I talk about how medicine robs women of our belief in our own perceptions, that I'm a prisoner of medicalization too. I didn't really believe yet that I was pregnant.

Every Saturday morning I sit on this table and say, "Hi, how are you all doing today? Is everybody OK? . . . You've had better days, right?

"My name is Anne. I'm going to go over the abortion procedure and answer any questions that you might have. The doctor should be here in about ten minutes, and then we'll go into the rooms, in the order that you got to the clinic. I'll be with you the whole time.

"The room looks like an ordinary exam room – have you all been to a gynecologist before? . . . No?

"This is a speculum. . . . This is a cannula," I say, holding up the thin plastic straw. "It's the instrument that we use to actually do the abortion. . . . " I pass it around the room.

"Does anyone have any questions? If you think of something later, be sure to ask."

Working at the clinic isn't my "real" job, it is just what

4

I do on Saturdays. I'm a writer. But Mark, the man I live with, and I had just moved to L.A., and I needed a place to be with other people, outside of myself, away from our house, a break from staring at the blinking cursor on my word processor screen.

And it is a break. When I am there, it is hard to remember that there is a world beyond these walls, hard to remember that this is just a fragment of my life.

Everyone tells me how good I am with the women. I hold their hands; I say, "Breathe slowly in and hold it. Breathe slowly out." My voice is low and gentle. "You're doing really well," I say. "We're almost done." By the end of the day, the rooms are thick with a smell like menstrual blood, but richer; the smell of the core of women. By the end of the day, the rooms are thick with mingled sadness and relief, and my head usually aches, and of course, my legs ache too.

A woman was whispering into the telephone, "This is Tran Le. I can't get out of the house." I could hear the sounds of children crying in the background. "My appointment's for nine o'clock... "

"Can you hang on for a second?" I said. A UPS man was knocking on the window separating the hallway from the reception area. I opened the window a crack and said, "Can I see your ID?"

"You'll have to get here as soon as you can," I said to the voice on the telephone, and turned back to the UPS man.

If the look he gave me were given free rein, it would have said, "Oh, Jesus Christ lady, what is your problem?" But it was just a hint, so that if I called his boss and complained about him, he could say with absolute conviction, "I wasn't doing anything. That woman is paranoid."

He held up his plastic ID card.

"Thank you," I said.

He thrust the metal clipboard and ballpoint pen at me. "Line 32."

"Just a sec," I said, checking to see who the package was addressed to and who it was from. I buzzed Roxanne. "I'm—"

"I know you're in a hurry." I hated to say this to him, but I hated even more to have him think that I got off on hassling UPS drivers. "This is an abortion clinic. We have to assume that every package we get is a bomb. I have to check and be sure the person it's addressed to is expecting this—"

"Oh." He looked at me. He looked at the parcel wrapped in brown paper in his hand.

I turned back to the telephone, "Roxanne, are you expecting a package from Dalton Medical Supply?... OK. It's here."

"It's fine. Sorry to hold you up."

Tran Le came to the clinic; she was only fifteen years old. It must have been her younger sisters and brothers I heard crying. She was worried about how long it would take, about getting home late and getting in trouble. The other women in the room suggested calling home, telling her mother that her friend's car had a flat tire. They let her go first, ahead of them, although she was the last to arrive.

When she undressed, her body seemed impossibly small. "Have you ever had a pelvic exam before?" Valerie, the doctor, asked her. She shook her head. Tears welled in her eyes.

She cried through the whole abortion while she clutched my hand and I murmured, "Breathe slowly, breathe, breathe."

When it was over, I said, "Can I give you a hug?" and I held her against me.

Another woman started crying when I was in the middle of my explanation. "I'm sorry," she said. "I had a saline abortion when I was six months pregnant.... I'm sorry."

6

"You know this will be very different," I said.

A saline abortion is done late in the second trimester. A woman actually goes into labor, and delivers a dead fetus.

"That must have been very difficult for you. . . . Did you at least have someone with you?"

"My mother," she sobbed.

She cried while I held her hand, and cried while her boyfriend told bad jokes, and cried through the whole abortion, despite two shots of Valium.

I go into the rooms with the women. I tell them to get undressed. I give them a gown if they want one. I hold their hands. We talk about where they go to school, or what they saw on television last night, or how scared they are. The vacuum aspirator gets wheeled in. The women put their feet in the stirrups; I hold their hands. "The doctor's going to insert the speculum now," I say. A plastic cannula, the aspirator is flipped on, the sucking machine, whooshing out cells that could have become another Sappho, another Margaret Thatcher, a Beethoven, a Hitler. Flip on the machine and a question mark-shaped embryo disappears in a wash of blood and a stab of pain.

Sometimes, when the women's faces started to blur together, when I could feel the sound of the aspirator being switched on, when the women squeezed my hand too hard, when the smell got to me, when it all just felt like too much, I would remember the first time I went to a gynecologist. It was 1969. I was seventeen years old. I was sitting in the examining room, dressed in my white cotton gown (this was before disposable ones), back before abortion was legal, sitting nervously waiting for my turn, when a woman's voice shrieked from the next room:

"No! I can't be pregnant! No! No!"

And she kept screaming, "No!" in that polite gynecologist's office with the pregnant women in the waiting room with their feet crossed at the ankle, the pregnant women reading *Ladies Home Journal* and *McCalls*, with looks on their faces that then were called serene but I think were often weariness and resignation, kept shrieking, "No," in the brick office building with the ivy growing up the walls, on tree-lined Waterman Street.

I could hear his voice too, a soothing deep male counterpoint, telling her – what? That someday she might come to love this child? That he couldn't recommend an abortionist, he'd risk his license, but that her friends might be able to? That with five children already, she'd hardly notice number six? That miscarriages are more frequent than you'd think? That he couldn't promise her anything, but given her blood pressure and her breakdown five years before, he might be able to get the board at the hospital to say that her life was endangered by the pregnancy? That lots of girls went into homes and had their babies and put them up for adoption and went on with their lives as if nothing had happened?

And she kept shrieking, "No! No! I can't be pregnant! I can't be pregnant! I can't be pregnant!"

About noon, I stuck my head out of an exam room and Arla caught sight of me and nodded her head.

"I'll be back in one second," I said to the woman sitting on the table, waiting for the doctor.

Roxanne came out of the sterile room, and hugged me. "I hope it's a girl."

Constance hugged me. "It'll be a girl."

Ginny relieved me in the room so I could go and call Mark. "Congratulations," she whispered, "I hope it's a girl."

I called Mark but he wasn't home. I left a message on

8

the tape. "Hi. It's me. I'm pregnant. God. Oh. I'll be home about four, I guess. Bye."

I picked up the pregnancy wheel that was lying on the desk, a gadget for calculating how far along a pregnant a woman is. My daughter would be born on September 7th, 1985. I'd already planned on a home birth. I imagined my daughter being born in the muted light of a September afternoon.

Arla came into the office and hugged me, saying, "It's about time." I had only been "trying" for three months, which was really not very long at all – except you tended to forget that when you worked in an abortion clinic and saw woman after woman with unwanted pregnancies, women who forgot their diaphragm just once, women who got pregnant on the pill. While there I was, going after pregnancy in true eighties style – taking my temperature with a basal thermometer each morning before I got out of bed, checking my cervical mucus, saying to Mark, "OK. We have to do it today."

Trying to get pregnant. How odd that phrase would have seemed to me ten years ago.

When I got home, Mark and I lay down together. It was nothing like the movies: he was not Cary Grant, I was not Myrna Loy. He did not look into my eyes and murmur, "Oh, my darling, I've never been happier."

I wondered if I looked as scared as he did. What had we done? Was I really, really, really sure this is what I want to do? Really, really, really sure? We were stuck with each other now.

How could I have felt so frantic about getting pregnant, so worried that I wouldn't, and now be so scared of being pregnant?

I lay there, and looked at Mark, and remembered all those conversations that we'd had in the dark, lying awake in bed. I was ready to have a child; he wasn't, not yet. I was thirty-three. How much longer could "not yet" go on for?

But what would our lives be like? What would it be like for me, who had polio as a child, to go through a pregnancy? What about money? We'd even figured out the cost on a piece of blue-lined paper, so much each month for diapers, so much for child care, the cost of a bigger place to live, with a second bedroom. We thought about everything, we thought it all through.

Mark's parents had both been killed in an automobile accident when he was twelve years old, and one night he said:

"I'm scared if we have a baby, it'll die," and began to cry.

"Don't worry," I said, "everything bad has already happened to us." We had suffered our tragedies, paid our dues: from here on out it would be easy sailing for the two of us.

2

Maybe that's not where this story really begins; maybe it really begins on a warm October morning in 1981.

I lived on the third floor of a railroad flat in San Francisco. When I was a kid growing up in Providence, Rhode Island, buildings like this were called triple deckers. Now a real estate agent would call this a Victorian: a long flight of stairs, high ceilings, a fireplace, a kitchen, not a kitchenette.

I was twenty-nine years old. In a few weeks I would be thirty, but still, I was twenty-nine. In the morning I was a writer, sitting at my second-hand green Selectric. At eleven every morning I finished writing and took a shower, got dressed, grabbed something to eat and by 11:25 I was headed down the long flight of stairs. In the afternoon I was a legal secretary, typing interrogatories and complaints. That morning I left a few minutes early so I could stop downstairs and take my clothes out of the dryer in the laundry room.

A few months before, I had read a notice in a newspaper for disabled people about a conference in the Midwest sponsored by *Rehabilitation Gazette* on post-polio respiratory problems and premature aging. I threw the newspaper under my bed.

I had polio in 1954, when I was three years old. I had crutches and braces as a child; surgery so many times that when someone asks me how often, I always have to count the thick caterpillar scars that crawl up my legs to figure it out. I walk with a cane now, a rolling walker, my body moving not with legs doing their own job, but a collective of shoulders and side and stomach – one whole side hitches up and then I toss my right leg forward.

I couldn't stop thinking about the notice. Every week, at the very end of my therapy session, I would say to Pat: "I worry about that – what do they mean – post-polio and premature aging?"

"I don't know," she would say with therapeutic stoicism.

"I should write them, shouldn't I?"

She would let a few seconds pass before she said, "We have to stop now."

I would walk out of her office resolving: I will go home and write the address on the envelope, an easy business letter, "I read your announcement about the conference... While I will not be able to attend, would appreciate more information about... Thank you in advance for your... Sincerely." A twenty-cent stamp, a lick of the envelope.

Finally I did it. I wrote the letter, signed my name, licked the stamp and pressed it with my fist, stroked the long flap of the envelope with my tongue.

That October morning in 1981, I went downstairs and there was a manila envelope lying face down against the mat. Not another rejected manuscript home so soon, I thought. I turned it over to see a return address that said, *Rehabilitation Gazette*, tore open the envelope and opened the magazine to read the lead story.

"In the past few years it has become increasingly obvious to post-polio people, doctors, and rehabilitation professionals, that when post-polio people approach the age of 40, they begin to face a host of problems more characteristic of old age than of middle age." I pictured a host of medical problems falling like anti-manna from the skies.

I had just stopped being a kid, I was just turning into an adult who (most of the time) returned her library books on time and balanced her checkbook and suddenly I was being told that I was about to enter old age? I was twenty-nine years old when I came down the steps; I aged a decade standing there on my front porch. "Many people find that increasing weakness forces them to change from canes and crutches to push wheelchairs; people who have previously used push chairs now need power chairs."

I stood on the front porch crying, pressing the heels of my hands against the sockets of my eyes. I don't want to be in a wheelchair, I don't want to be in a wheelchair, I don't want to be in a wheelchair.

I wanted to throw my cards down on the table: I fold. Please deal me a new hand, a new body. Give me a new struggle, I'm sick of this one.

I shoved the *Gazette* into my purse and went out to the laundry room. I folded my clothes warm from the dryer, matching cuff against cuff, smoothing out creases; crying. Considered going back up the stairs, asking Beth to call work: "Anne's sick, she won't be in today." But I wanted the comfort of routine, of my fingers typing someone else's words, so I drove to the office.

The article said that those who were the best patients fared the worst. Polio rehabilitation was aggressive — long hours devoted to physical therapy, straining to get damaged nerves to function again. It was the Protestant ethic gone wild: the more you worked, the better you would get. The more you suffered, the more you gained. Now the theory was that we had been "over-rehabilitated" — that our weakened nerves broke down because they were forced to do too much.

When I was in high school, I used to walk home from school every day, out of breath before I had made it to the end of the first block. All my clothes were stained with gigantic circles of perspiration under the arms because I was always, even in the dead of a New England winter, dripping sweat by the time I got home. I always threw my coat on the floor because I was just too tired to walk the few steps to the hall closet. My legs were always aching, and I was always striving, straining, reaching to do more.

After work, I went to the medical library at San Francisco General to find the medical journal articles cited in the *Rehabilitation Gazette*. The man behind the counter was eating a peach, the juice dribbling down into his beard. I stacked my dimes up on the edge of the xerox machine and copied "Forme Fruste Amytrophic Lateral Scelerosis or Post-Polio Deterioration?" and "Late Motor Neuron Degeneration." I sat down with my xeroxes and underlined the words I didn't understand: *fasciculations; Babinski's sign; extrapyramidal.*

I read case histories: "This male patient was 10 years old at the time of his first admission to our clinic in 1922 with a diagnosis of 'infantile paralysis.'... In October 1965, he returned with no medical problem other than increasing weakness after some 40 years stability. A politician, he had noted for two years trouble getting his right hand up to the proper position for shaking, and a weakening of his golf grip.... Four years after he started to weaken, he had to use a wheelchair. After five years, only his wife and secretary could understand his speech, and records indicate that his wife spent 2½ hours per day feeding him. He last was seen at the Mayo Clinic in June 1969 and could not tent his cheek with his tongue, could not flex his neck against gravity, and had progression of both weakness and atrophy...."

The word "progressive" was no longer a political description that floated somewhere between liberal and radical. It meant progressive illness, progressive condition, progressive deterioration.

For the first time in years, I went to see a doctor about my polio. There hadn't seemed any point before, because all I ever heard was that I was "holding my own." I had to wait three weeks for an appointment, and every day I woke up and thought, "Twenty more days," then "Nineteen more days."

The first thing he asked me was not what year I had polio, but what I did. I'm a secretary I said, but really a writer. Fiction, short stories, working on a novel. We talked about writers; he asked me who I liked. Tillie Olsen, Grace Paley, I'd loved a few stories that had been in the *New Yorker* by a writer named Stephanie Vaughn.

"Oh, Stephanie," he said, "I went to college with her."

He was so sweet, a doctor who read, who read fiction; I felt blessed.

I told him I was concerned because of what I had been reading lately about polio. He said that doctors were thinking differently about polio now, looking at the effects on the whole body, becoming concerned about joint and energy conservation.

We went over my surgeries.

"Let's see, I had surgery four – no, five – times."

He touched the scars on my legs. "A bone graft here?" he asked.

"I think. I was so young, I really don't remember."

"And this one?"

"A tendon transplant."

He drew "x"s on my back with a blue ball point pen and told me I had scoliosis: My spine, instead of being straight, bent slightly to the right. I told him I was worried about my lungs, my breathing. He said, "Don't worry about your lungs, worry about your right arm."

He told me to start using a cane; he sent me to physical therapy, for x-rays on my back.

He told me about a local conference for people who were post-polio that was going to be held in a few weeks in Berkeley.

*

At that conference in Berkeley I sat for the first time in my life in a room filled with other disabled people. I remember how nervous I felt. Mark was sitting next to me, and I felt glad to have a blond-haired, able-bodied lover at my side. I'd always gone to "regular" schools; I'd been mainstreamed before there was a word for it. I had moved through the world as a normal person with a limp, and no thank you, I didn't need any help, I could manage just fine. And, no, I was nothing like "them." I wasn't whiny, or needy or self-pitying. By the time I sat in that room, I'd shed enough of that baggage to know I wasn't "supposed" to think those things. So I just sat there, feeling what a psychologist would call free-floating anxiety.

I remember Judy Heumann, a disability rights activist, coming into the room. Her way was blocked by some chairs, and to this day I see the image of her, plowing the green plastic chairs out of her way. It was both shocking (it seemed so rude) and deeply satisfying: they were in her way. She got them out of her way.

I felt such commonality with the other people there who'd had polio. It was as if I had been living all my life in a foreign land, speaking a language that was not my native tongue. Here I was at last among people who understood, who understood without elaboration, explanation.

One of the speakers on a panel of people who were post-polio was a man who had been left only with the use of one arm. One day, when he was on his way to his van, he dropped his keys. He bent over from his electric wheelchair to pick them up and discovered that he couldn't straighten himself up: he'd suddenly lost the use of his "good" arm. Another woman, also in an electric wheelchair, spoke. She had a normal-looking body (I thought it, I'll say it); she wasn't twisted with scoliosis or contracted. She said she used to get around with just a cane.

She looked almost normal, like me, I thought.

I wanted to be able to embrace this community. And I wanted to be able to walk away from it, too. I wanted to be able to return to the world where I more or less passed for normal. Normal. Pass. Loaded words.

And then there was the fear. I didn't want what had happened to them to happen to me. I didn't want to grow weaker, to do less. To me, the words that followed next in that sequence were "be less."

3

The events of that fall triggered something inside me. I wanted to have a baby. I wanted something perfect to come out of my imperfect body. I wanted a child, with a child's smooth skin, not a scar, a mark, a blemish. I never imagined myself as having a son, only a daughter: I wanted to make myself anew. I needed to have control over my body: instead of letting it grow more frail, letting it lose its power, I wanted to make it grow, to do more, not less.

I wanted my power to be *physical*. People used to say to my friend Mary, a quadriplegic, "You still have your mind." She would say, "I still have my body." The world tells me to divorce myself from my flesh, to live in my head. Once somebody showed me, excitedly, a postage stamp from Nicaragua: a man in a wheelchair, working alone, peering into a microscope. There's a U.S. postage stamp that's almost exactly the same. It's always someone working alone, preferably male, brilliant, fleshless, a Mind. I didn't want to be alone; I didn't want to be fleshless.

For weeks I went around infatuated with the idea of having a child, looking at baby clothes and nursery furniture in store windows. I didn't consciously plan to get pregnant, but I went a month without using birth control.

I found out I was pregnant on December 31st. In San Francisco, everyone throws their office calendars down into the streets on the day before New Year. I remembered shuffling through all those dead days of August and June, Mays and Octobers gone by on my way to work.

The clinic where I had gone to have the pregnancy test had told me to call them at two. At one, I sat at my desk at work and ran my finger down the listing in the phone book:

Buena Vista Annex Alternative Elementary School
Buena Vista Church of Christ
Buena Vista Farms
Buena Vista Liquors
Buena Vista Winery
Buena Vista Women's Services, and dialed that number.

Yes, I said, I can hold for a minute; hope the other line doesn't ring. "This is Anne Finger, I had a blood test there the other day. Do you have the results yet?"

"Anne Singer?"

"No. Finger. Like what's on the end of your hand."

"Oh, Finger," she said, flipping through files. "Urine or blood?"

"Blood."

"Here it is. Your test was positive."

"Positive?"

"You're pregnant."

Me, pregnant? When I was a child, the girl games—dress-ups, dolls—always seemed just that, games. The real self was the tomboy self, the climber of rock piles and the collector of skeletons of mice and the skull of a cow. How could I be pregnant?

Mark and I thought about it over the weekend. We walked up 24th Street; it was blossoming babies. I skipped the New Year's champagne; I bought a gallon of milk in a plastic bottle. I'd wanted a child ever since I was in my mid-twenties. But—I had exactly five dollars in my checking account; ten dollars in my savings account. When Mark said on Monday morning that he really wasn't ready to have a child, I was relieved to have him slice through my

19

web of ambiguities and fears and desires. I couldn't have a child just as a balm for me. What I wanted was the dream of perfection, not the reality of a child.

I called Kaiser, the HMO I belonged to, that Monday morning. The receptionist said I couldn't get an appointment with my own nurse practitioner for ten days, so I scheduled an appointment with the first available doctor.

The first available doctor, I realized, was available because no one wants to see him.

He walked into the room and started firing questions: "Who does that cane belong to? How did you get pregnant? Who are you?" (The last question was directed at Mark.) He didn't wait for me to answer, just rat-a-tat-tat. The machine-gun approach to medicine.

He asked me when I'd had polio; I said, when I was not quite three. He gave me a withering look: "What year?" Orthopedic surgery? How many times? Five or six. Anything else wrong with you? Heart troubles, epilepsy, anything like that? What about your family? Anything wrong with your family? No, I said, there's nothing wrong with my family.

Then he rattled off a speech at me, before I signed the consent form, like a 33 record speeded up to 45: "You understand there's always some risk when we do surgery when you have a tooth pulled there's a risk of death and statistically it's about the same as when you have an abortion O.K. are you sure there's nothing else wrong with you?"

He gave me a pelvic so rough I cramped for the rest of the day and an appointment for an abortion in three weeks time. (There was a waiting list.) He walked out and slammed the door.

Every morning I woke up sick after having slept later than I had ever slept in my adult life; every day I came home from work and faced that long flight of stairs up to our flat not believing I could possibly make it to the top. Mt. Everest, the Matterhorn, Denali: up I climbed, and up. I was always falling down: flat on my back twice on concrete, my knee giving out, again and again I tumbled down. A hormone, I remembered someone saying, that loosens up the pelvic area, loosens all your joints. That's why women's feet get bigger after they have their first child. But if you don't have normal muscles supporting your joints, they get floppy and weak and give way.

After three weeks of falling down and counting the days left to go till my appointment, I got to Kaiser at six in the morning. They had given me this mimeographed sheet; it said, "Wear no make-up, nail polish, wigs or jewelry. Be sure to bring your health plan card with you." There were five of us having abortions together. We had to take off our clothes and put on paper gowns, paper caps over our hair, paper booties on our feet. We shuffled down the hall together, almost identical, plain, with our bare hands and bare faces.

The nurse rolled us over one by one and said to each of us, "This won't hurt, just a pinch... " as she stuck the needle in our butts, "This won't hurt, just a pinch. . . . "

I was woozy with drugs as they wheeled me into the operating room. The doctor – she must have been an intern, a first-year resident – started to whine to the slightly older doctor sitting in the corner, "I can't find her cervix. I can't find her cervix."

On the O.R. table, I am a child again, a six-year-old child, and I cannot –

Wait. Stop. I don't want this to be happening to me, you said sleep, Mommy. You said they will put you to sleep and this is not sleep, this is like dying. No, not like dying, like being murdered. Poison gas, the fumes swirling down your throat. You fight but they are holding you down, and there are so many of them and you are just a child.

No. You are not a child any more. You are not a six-year-old who had polio three and a half years before, having surgery to fuse your ankle, stretch your Achilles tendon. You are not a six-year-old child wheeled into the operating room wide awake, under the glaring hundred-eyed lamp, to have a mask held over your face and the swirling fumes pull you down.

You are a woman now. This is an abortion. I have chosen this. I am an adult now. I have a job, my job pays for Kaiser. I am having an abortion at Kaiser. This is mine. I have earned it. I have chosen it.

The room dissolves and there is nothing but pain at the core of me. There is no bright light above me, no woman with her hair pulled back in a flowered operating room cap, no intern scooting between my legs, no doctor sitting in the corner. Just pain.

They are yelling at me, "Relax, relax," because my right leg is shaking. It is unsupported in the stirrup, and I can't form the words to tell them, it's not that I'm not relaxed, I'm post-polio, that's what the shaking's coming from, someone needs to hold my leg.

"Relax," they shout at me, through the IV valium.

The woman in the flowered cap gives me another injection. I thought I would be able to do the relaxation breathing that I know from yoga during my abortion, but the drugs make me too out of it to concentrate.

In the recovery room, the five of us who have had abortions are lined up along one wall. Along the opposite wall are women who are recovering from drugged childbirth. I wake up to hear someone shouting through the anesthetic fog at another woozy woman: "You have a son. You have a little boy. You have a son."

4

I just couldn't shake the feelings from that abortion. It wasn't that it seemed wrong to me. But why had it been such an alienating experience?

I saw my friend Lily in New York that summer. She'd had an abortion not too long before. "They had Muzak piped in through the whole clinic," she said. "Oh, God, I'll never forget that." She pasted a fake smile on her face and nodded her head back and forth in a sing-song rhythm.

My abortion, which after all meant my right to my self, had felt like just the opposite: a surrendering of myself to medical control. It was symbolized by that shuffle down a hospital corridor with four other women, all of us dressed alike in garments of disposable paper, bare of all adornment. All about to share the same experience, but none of us even knowing each other's names.

I wrote a story about my abortion experience, and ended up by imagining a home abortion, like a home birth. "Mark would play the guitar," I wrote, "while Susan read bittersweet poems by Pablo Neruda or Anne Sexton."

A few months later, I joined an abortion rights group, the Committee to Defend Reproductive Rights. Since I was developing some disability consciousness, I casually offered to do a talk for one of their monthly meetings on disability and reproductive rights.

I was pretty naive. I didn't think anything I said was going to be particularly controversial.

I had a lot to learn.

That evening, as we all sat on folding chairs in the Women's Building, I talked about the history of the eugenics movement, especially in terms of disabled people, and how it had reached its terrible fulfillment in Nazi Germany, first in the forcible sterilization of disabled people and then in genocide – which began, not in the concentration camps, but in the hospitals and mental institutions of Germany.

I could feel the tension level in the room rising as I spoke about disability and sexuality. And when I started talking about how the reproductive rights movement was sometimes guilty of exploiting fears about disability when it argued for abortion because of fetal defect, things got really strained. I said that we could defend women's right to have an abortion in such a situation without acting as if there were no other possible choice.

I went on to talk about a recent instance of a child who had been born with Down's Syndrome and a defect in his gastrointestinal tract which prevented him from absorbing nourishment. Without surgery, the child would starve to death. The parents and the doctors decided not to perform the surgery – reasoning that life with Down's Syndrome was not worth living – and the child did in fact starve to death. This happened despite the fact that many people came forward and offered to adopt the child. (Infants and young children with Down's Syndrome can usually be placed in adoptive homes quite easily.)

The case became a *cause célèbre* with right-wing, anti-abortion forces, who used legal avenues and public pressure in an attempt to save the child's life. They argued that this was the logical outcome of abortion rights. Because the parents' names were not released to the public, the child was called "Baby Doe" in court documents. The case, and others like it, came to be known as the "Baby Doe" issue.

Most reproductive rights activists took a knee-jerk position against the anti-abortionists, advocating "parental choice" and "the right to privacy" without examining the very real disability issues involved.

When the discussion period began, I felt like a heretic. Wasn't it a terrible burden on women to have to care for disabled children? Shouldn't disabled infants be allowed to escape the misery of their lives? "I was glad when my daughter was born quote-unquote normal – do I have to feel guilty for that?"

What it all boiled down to was, did I really think that disabled people were as good as everyone else? Was I really saying that a disabled life was worth living?

I was too stunned to respond to them very well. What seemed obvious to me – that a disabled life *was* worth living; that our lives weren't endless misery – seemed dubious at best to them.

I remembered a dream that I have had occasionally throughout my life. I stand up before a group of people and begin to deliver a talk or perhaps read a story. After a minute or two, I notice that people are shifting uncomfortably in their seats; then they begin to nudge each other and whisper. I overhear someone: "What is she saying?" Then I hear my own voice. I am speaking, but what is coming out of my mouth is not words, but gobbledygook, jumbled random syllables that make no sense. I keep trying to talk, but people are starting to laugh at the nonsense coming out of my mouth.

At the meeting it was all coming too fast for me to feel much of anything, but by the time I got home I was furious, miserable. When I lay down in bed that night, my mind raced: How could they be so – smug, that was the word. So certain that what they had always known/assumed was right? I'd always thought that progressive people just hadn't had much of a chance to become acqauinted with disability issues; that once they had a little bit of education, they'd clean up their act. I expected lip service, condescension, liberalism – but certainly not hostility.

And something else, too: deeper, not yet formed into words: these women are like the people you have lived among all your life: you always assumed that those around you saw you as their equal. They are telling you no: we suffer your presence.

Chris Finch, one of the women in the Committee to Defend Reproductive Rights, was a nurse who worked in the neonatal intensive care unit at San Francisco General. She kept talking about how we torture babies in NICUs, and telling me in a mournful voice about a baby with an Apgar of 0 who was resuscitated. (An Apgar score is quick method of rating a newborn, on a scale of 0 to 10, by evaluating such things as heart rate, respiration and muscle tone.) I got the impression from the way she spoke that the child was doomed to be a nothing, a few steps up from brain dead.

Chris gave me an article to read from a journal called Neonatal Network. The narrator pretended to be a premature newborn speaking. The child was on a warming bed, she was receiving one hundred percent oxygen through a ventilator; she had an umbilical artery catheter and an intravenous line in her scalp. She was being given a drug to paralyze her. She described her tortuous and difficult first twenty-four hours. Over and over again, the newborn "asks": Is my life going to be worth living? If I live I will be handicapped and dependent – why are they saving me? The article ends with the baby repeating, "I want to die. I want to die. I want to… "

The article angered me. It pretended to speak with the

voice of the child, when in fact it was articulating the concerns of the author.

That wasn't the only thing about the article that was disturbing. The piece counted on me having a gut reaction to this technology. It described strange procedures and expected me to recoil in horror at the description of this baby trussed up with leads and lines. And I did. But I've learned over the years that my gut has been well socialized along with the rest of me: I've recoiled at men in women's clothes; at the sight of a woman with severe facial burns. I've learned to look at those things that I "automatically" react against and to ask myself why. What was at the heart of my reaction against all this technology?

Chris took me to see the neonatal intensive care unit at General. The NICU was empty. She showed me the strange square beds with the clear plastic sides and the boxy machines overhead that were lying ready and waiting. We walked into the special care nursery, adjacent to the NICU. The first baby we saw was lying alone in his plastic incubator, shaking and shaking and shaking. I had never seen a child in so much pain and my first thought was, I change my mind. I take back everything I said. This is horrible.

"He's going through heroin withdrawal," she said. "He's in pretty good shape. His mother was getting prenatal care, and eating well."

I wondered why no one was holding him.

"Addicts' babies are so jittery that being touched bothers them even more."

A three-pound premie, covered with dark downy hair; a baby who was meant to be an abortion. "The doctor didn't know what he was doing – really, the woman was too late for an abortion. He put in too much laminaria – you know what they are? – seaweed strands that absorb

27

moisture and dilate the cervix. She dilated fully and delivered at home–"

I stared at that sleeping infant who was meant to be a late abortion and instead was a very premature birth. My friend was saying that the baby may be blind and deaf as a result. I think: I will go home and talk to Mark and we'll adopt this baby. I want to fix it, erase the pain of staring at this child.

I think Chris thought that seeing the NICU would upset me so much that it would change my opinions, shock me out of what she saw as my naivete. It disturbed me, but it didn't change what I believed.

I wrote up the talk I had given to CDRR. It was published–after a fight about its political content–in the feminist newspaper, *Off Our Backs*. (The editors thought it would make women feel guilty about their abortions.) A different version of it appeared in the book, *Test-Tube Women: What Future for Motherhood?* I started getting asked to appear on panels and give speeches. It was strange to realize that only a few months before I had been sitting at that conference in Berkeley, nervous to be surrounded by so many people in wheelchairs.

5

In March of 1984, Janet Gallagher, a lawyer who headed a reproductive rights program at Hampshire College, called a meeting in New York to try and iron out some of the differences among feminists on the "Baby Doe" issue as well as on amniocentesis and selective abortion.

In New York, I am a child again, not knowing north from south, east from west; trusting in those who knew; moving through a too-big world. I climb into taxis and read from slips of paper: 65 Fifth Avenue, 117th and Broadway, and off we fly, weaving through wide New York streets and racing yellow lights.

On Sunday morning we meet in the women's center at Barnard, sitting around a big wooden table, drinking coffee and herbal tea from styrofoam cups.

Janet says, "Well, I thought the way we'd begin was to go around and introduce ourselves and say a little bit about what we've done or thought about these things. . . . "

"I'm Deborah Kaplan. I'm an attorney with DREDF" (pronounced "dread-if") "that's the Disability Rights Education and Defense Fund – in Berkeley. Well." She takes a deep breath. "I was born prematurely – three months ahead of schedule, but perfectly formed. I spent the first three months of my life in an incubator. I've often had a deep feeling of aloneness and I wonder if that stems from those months of being in an incubator." Debbie's eyes thicken, and a few tears roll down her cheeks.

"I wasn't disabled though until I was twenty, and when I think of some of the misconceptions about disability that I had prior to the time that I broke my neck, it really frightens me. The difference between what I imagined disability to be like and what it actually was like was enormous. It frightens me to think that people who know nothing about disability make a decision to abort on that basis."

Barbara Katz Rothman, sitting next to Debbie, turns to her and says, "I'm so glad you started crying. I always cry when I think about this stuff.

"For the past two years, I've been doing research on amniocentesis and how it affects women's experience of their pregnancies. Well, it all started when I was invited to give a talk at a clinic that provides prenatal diagnosis services for low-income women. I had to write this dinky little ten minute talk and it took me just weeks and weeks to write. Everyone was saying, well, of course, this technology is available to middle-class women, it has to be made available to women who aren't middle-class.

"But I'm not so sure. I hate this technology," she says. "Somewhere, sometime there might be a culture that's able to handle it—just like somewhere, sometime there might be a culture that could handle nuclear power. But it isn't this culture. . . . "

She adds, "My mother was very young when I was born. If abortion had been available she might have taken that option. Of course, in some sense it wouldn't have been *me*. Who I am is more than just a collection of cells, genetic memory."

Adrienne Asch leans her head back. "I was a premie. My blindness is a result of RLF, from the oxygen in the incubator. . . . For a long time they thought that they could control the levels of oxygen, and infants wouldn't go blind.

There was an article a few weeks ago in *The New York Times* saying that now doctors are realizing that some blindness is inevitable, and many were thinking that it was better for these kids to die than to be blind. I was just appalled at that attitude of it's better to be dead than to be blind."

She turns to Rayna, then says, "Oh. I forgot to say: I teach here at Barnard and I work for the New York Human Rights Commission."

Rayna Rapp is eight months pregnant: a tiny woman with a huge belly. She wears jeans and a flannel shirt, nothing with tucks and bows that disguise her shape. "Well, as most of you know, the way I got involved in this issue was that I had an abortion at five months when I discovered that the fetus I was carrying had Down's.

"I talk about this as a death, and sometimes people are critical of me for using that word, but to Mike and me it felt like death.

"Emotionally, it was a very, very difficult experience for me. It was made worse by the isolation I felt. I have always tried to understand my personal struggles in a social context, and so I began to try to make contact with other women who had also had abortions following amniocentesis.

"It was a strange decision for me—the decision to abort—because as an anthropologist I have spent most of my life struggling against notions of biological determinism—and yet, at that moment in my life I found myself making this decision based solely on biological criteria."

Ruth Hubbard's long straight hair is pure white. "I'm a professor of biology at Harvard. My family fled to this country from Austria when I was a child, after Hitler invaded." She still has a trace of a German accent. "That experience has left me with a deep distrust of the state.

"I myself gave birth to two children when I was well past thirty. No one told me that was too old to be having a child, or that I was high risk, and thank God I didn't think of myself that way. This was back before Thalidomide, but as a biologist I was always very wary of any kind of technological intervention during pregnancy – I avoided all drugs, even then, back when pregnant women were being dosed with DES and other drugs.

"My problems with amniocentesis – well, prenatal screening – stem mostly from my concern about how it's recreating eugenic thinking. We act as if we can look at a gene and say, 'Ah-ha, this gene causes this behavior, this disability,' when in fact the interactions between genes and the environment are enormously complex. It moves our focus from the environmental causes of disabilities – which are terrifying and increasing daily – to individual, genetic ones."

Janet's turn is next. She is on the board of Catholics for a Free Choice, came to the women's movement from the Catholic left, was in a novitiate herself, "but only for nine months… It's always been interesting to me, working in the abortion rights movement, when personally I doubt I would ever choose abortion.

"I'm from an Irish Catholic family of six – only six, as we said in our neighborhood – but my mother had eleven pregnancies. I bring to this the knowledge that had my mother had more control over her life, she would probably never have given birth to me."

Janet's mother had miscarriages, and children who died at birth or in early infancy. "I remember my father lined us up in the hallway, and one after another, we went in, and he told us that the baby had died. . . . Sometimes I feel as if my political work is haunted by ghosts, the ghosts of those miscarried fetuses, of those dead children. . . . but I think too we do the best work politically when we're doing work that really tears at us."

Janet looks like the Irish Catholic girls who lived near us when I was growing up – girls whose last names were Mahoney or Harrington or McCormick, and whose first names were Claire and Kathleen. I like looking at her face because it makes me feel that after all these years of change there is still something that connects me to that big old house on Larch Street, those summer evenings watching the baseball games at the old School for the Deaf.

It's my turn last. "Well, I'm disabled. I wasn't born disabled, but had polio when I was three years old, and my earliest memories are of that—I don't remember a time when I wasn't disabled. I believe very strongly that we have to protect the lives of disabled infants. To say that a disabled person is just not worth as much as another person, or doesn't have the same rights because they're disabled is frightening to me.

"At the same time – I too question much of the technology that is used. I went to visit a neonatal special care unit and I looked at all that stuff and said, 'This place was not designed by babies.'

"When I was a child in the hospital, I was subjected to things that were really inhumane. My mother was only allowed to see me for an hour a day—this was when I was three years old. I remember the bell ringing at four o'clock, when visiting hours were over, and the sound of children wailing that followed." I am crying now, and so is everyone else in the room.

Barbara says, "If you had been my child, I would have killed you before I let that happen. I would have killed myself too."

My heart stops. She is telling me I should not be alive. It is my old fear come true: That if you talk about the pain, people will say, see, it isn't worth it. You would be better off dead.

My heart stops. I feel violated. She had no right to say that to me, anymore than I would have a right to say to Rayna: "I would never have done that. I would never have aborted a fetus with Down's."

I get up and leave the room. I am angry. I need time to let my heart start beating again. I wander around for a few minutes in the hallway, reading the notices on the bulletin board. I go to the bathroom.

When I come back in, Adrienne is talking about the pain that infants experience. Listen to a baby screaming with colic, she is saying: that is a child in misery. We're used to colic, we know the baby will outgrow it: this is everyday suffering. But the infant does not know it. She has been torn from the gentleness of her mother's womb to a world that is strange and terrifying. "Is the pain of the infant in an NICU really so different? It's more difficult for those watching, because to us it seems unnatural, and we bring to it all our associations of hospitals and medical procedures as things *we* have learned to think of as frightening and painful."

Debby says: "I've been realizing over the last few weeks of talking about this – with other disabled people at DREDF and with some of the parents of disabled kids who are at DREDF – that there's a very big difference depending on who you identify with – the parent or the child. I identify strongly with the child."

Barbara talks about a book she has read, *The Long Dying of Baby Andrew*. It was written by the parents of a child who was born very prematurely – a baby due in April who was born in December, weighing less than two pounds. In the book, the parents describe the harrowing days and weeks and months of watching their son, who was almost certainly going to die, being subjected to an unending series of medical procedures. He lived in a world dominated by machines, breathing with a respirator, having blood transfusions, being resuscitated again and again; finally dying without having left the hospital, at the age of six months.

I say, "That's different, using high tech medicine to prolong dying." The medical treatment needed by the baby born in Indiana with Down's syndrome, for instance, wasn't particularly high tech or experimental. It wasn't a question of treatment of a dying child, but of a child who would almost certainly live – and have a disability. Different maybe than what I see as "the issue" here, but still an issue. If ninety percent of premies under 1000 grams die, do you not treat any of them? Do you treat all of them, knowing that you will learn from your mistakes and other children will benefit from their slow deaths? It seems wrong to me to totally disregard the needs and feelings of parents, but suppose parents don't want medical treatments for their child because they want a perfect child – or even because they're worried about money, a legitimate concern, but hardly one to base a life and death decision on.

Barbara talks about her fear that "Baby Doe regulations" will be used to restrict childbearing rights. These were regulations put out by the Federal government, using the authority of Section 504 of the Rehabilitation Act of 1973, commonly called "the civil rights act for disabled people." The rules stated that handicapped infants in institutions receiving Federal funds had to be fed and cared for on a non-discriminatory manner – i.e., that a situation like the one which had occurred in Bloomington where the child with Down's Syndrome was allowed to starve to death – would be considered discrimination.

Many doctors are eager to restrict women's childbearing rights, some of them even saying that women who give birth outside of medical jurisdiction should be charged with child abuse. Barbara had both her children at home, and wrote a book about home birth. For a few minutes, we sink into one of those "Where do you draw the line?" discussions. When does the fetus-infant start to have legal rights?

"At birth," Janet says.

"When at birth," Barbara asks. "Crowning? Birth of the placenta?"

Adrienne asks Barbara, "If you say that parents of disabled children have the right to make those decisions, then don't the parents of non-disabled children have the same rights, to refuse medical treatment?"

"Yes," says Barbara.

"What about a Jehovah's Witness who doesn't believe in blood transfusions? Should their child be allowed to die?" Adrienne asks.

"Yes," Barbara says, slowly and reluctantly.

"And parents who beat their children?"

"Yes," she says, even more slowly and reluctantly.

We take a break. Rayna and Adrienne go out for fruit and bagels. When we come back, we start talking about amniocentesis.

Since her own experience, Rayna has been studying the issue of prenatal screening. She says that a lot of women she talks with cite "practical" reasons for having the test, because the same test that reveals the presence of Down's also reveals the sex. You can decorate the nursery in pink or blue; people will know what to get you as a shower gift. Sex roles are now beginning even before birth.

Women also sometimes receive "ambiguous diagnoses." Barbara tells of one woman she interviewed who was told that her fetus had a "fifteen percent chance" of becoming schizophrenic because of a chromosomal abnormality.

"That's a bullshit diagnosis," Rayna says.

"But it's what she had to go on."

As genetic testing becomes more and more "sophisticated," fetuses will get diagnosed as having predispositions to all sorts of diseases: cancer, arthritis, heart disease, manic-depression.

"How," Barbara asks, "do you look into the future? My father died of cancer when he was in his twenties. Suppose my father's mother could have been told when she was pregnant that her son would die painfully of cancer when he was a young man and leave his children fatherless? How could she have said, yes, I'll bring this child into the world to face that?"

We are aching over prenatal diagnosis of Down's but there are things that are so much harder.

Huntington's Chorea – the disease that killed Woody Guthrie – a rare genetic disorder, always fatal, that strikes at midlife, can now be diagnosed prenatally. Before it kills its victims (the political voice in my head says, don't say victims, think of some neutral way of saying that, say "before it kills those who carry its gene" and then I think no, victim is the right word) – before it kills its victims, they suffer through loss of control over their bodily functions, loss of speech. Now the genetic marker for Huntington's has been found. A woman with a family history of Huntington's can elect to have amniocentesis and then an abortion. Or she can choose not to. But she must choose. Her children can choose to be tested and find out if they will develop the disease or not. They can wonder or they can know.

Now you also have to choose not to choose.

You can always take refuge in talking about doing what's natural. But what is natural? Eating oranges in March in New York? And yes, doctors are playing God when they hook a baby up to a respirator – but they're playing God too when they write a prescription for an antibiotic to cure an infection that could well have killed fifty years ago.

At the end of the meeting, we sit holding hands in silence. I think, I am so glad I am a woman. I think of all the men I know – men who are not "masculine," men I like and respect, men I have learned tremendous amounts from politically – and I cannot imagine one of them able to sit around this table with us and feel the closeness we are feeling now. Not some sappy, superficial coming together, the result of a too-cheerful therapist having said, "Let's all give each other a hug," but true intimacy, born of commonality and difference, born of our shared commitment to women, born of our willingness to sit with each other's truth.

6

When I flew back to California, my connecting flight was late, and I ended up spending most of the night in the airport. They have armrests along the upholstered benches now, I suppose so that homeless people can't come in and stretch themselves out. Everything is bolted to the floor too, so you can't even drag another bench over to put your feet up on.

I didn't sleep well. When I got on the plane, it was almost empty and so I got a pillow and blanket from the flight attendant and stretched out. Still, I didn't really sleep, although I flickered close to sleep as I flew across the country.

Lying there on the plane, I think that probably the single most important fact about my life is that I rode a bus to school every morning and home from school every afternoon when I was a kid. I would sit on the back of the bus, and shut my eyes and daydream or just stare out the window. I was always sad when the bus turned onto Lake Moraine Road and I would have to get off. There was something about that state of being neither here nor there that was magic. Way on into early adulthood, I would drive aimlessly in cars to get some of that same sensation back. I wonder when it was that my life became so

deliberate and busy that I stopped loving that state of being in between where I had come from and where I was
going, and became in such a hurry to get places.

There on the nearly empty plane, half-asleep, I get
back to that state, a little. I keep thinking about what Janet
said, about how we do our best political work from the
place where hurt and questioning come together.

I think how odd it is that I work in a movement for reproductive control when randomness lies at the very heart
of reproduction. The woman who sits at the keyboard,
writing her words, exists because of a chance union of egg
and sperm. If my parents hadn't made love the evening I
was conceived, if my mother had shifted her hips
slightly – another sperm would have reached that egg, and
I never would have been.

I have three sisters and a brother of flesh and how
many more who are ghost-sisters, possibilities, im-
possibilities? I think for a minute about those daughters of
randomness who never were and never will be, and their
non-existence starts to seem as miraculous as my own existence.

Perhaps it is because I had polio that I have always
been fascinated by chance. My mother and oldest sister
were affected by the polio virus too, but for them – as for
most people – the disease was not paralytic. They had stiff
necks and upset stomachs: a summer flu. But in my case,
the virus happened to infect my spinal cord, and left me
partially paralyzed. It happened not to travel all the way
up my spinal cord and kill me.

The flight attendant rolls a cart down the aisle, and I
slip up a little more towards wakefulness.

I think about my great-grandmother who died a few
days after giving birth to my grandmother, probably from
puerperal fever, an epidemic caused by doctors who
carried germs from one birthing woman to another. A
month before she died, she wrote to my great-grandfather:

40

"Dear Will,

If I should have a girl baby and die will you get a good person to take care of it... (if a boy you must do just as you like about where to put it or who to care for it). If you get married to some one take good care of my little baby and try to teach it to be good... I want my baby to have everything that is mine if it lives.... Will, if I haven't a baby send the piano to father or mother... "

I think of all that we have won in the century since Annie Simmons, delivered of a girl child by the hands that killed her, faced the possibility of her own death and the death of her child with such frank courage.

Another letter, not from my own family, written a few decades later, in 1910, reads: "His wife and little ones are well although I am sorry to say there has been another little girl born. To me it seems very sad, seeing they have had so much trouble in their young lives, to bring more children into the world appears to one only short of a crime. But I suppose it will go on till the time comes when the birth of children will be hailed with joy instead of sadness."

That was seventy-nine years ago, not so long. We have won so much. We have made it so that the birth of children is hailed with joy. At least for some of us.

Each victory sets the stage for the next round of struggle.

We have set the stage for this new round of struggle: the struggles that arise from expecting our births to be joyful occasions.

But how do we, people who believe in the possibility, the necessity, of change, how do we grapple with the reality that we cannot eliminate all pain and suffering?

Once, Arthur Koestler was speaking with some Communist Party members about what the world would be like when Communism was achieved. They said that all suffering would be eliminated. What, he asked, about the pain caused by a trolley car running over a child. Ah, one of them said, after the revolution, trolley cars would no longer run over children.

That may seem laughable; but I have heard people talk about a right to have healthy children – as if we could legislate biology.

I mull over the things we talked about at the meeting. It's true, I think I wouldn't abort if my child were going to have Down's syndrome or spina bifida. But if I were faced with the possibility of a child with Tay Sachs – a progressive neurological disorder that causes death in early childhood – then I would have an abortion. I know, too, how easy it is to think: I would do this, I wouldn't do that, when you're not living the reality.

I have the places where I draw my lines about what I would and would not do; and other people, people I respect, have different lines. But I'm aware too of how social pressure can work to keep people in line: how when a technology is available it becomes harder and harder not to utilize it – "to take advantage of it." If you are over thirty-five and pregnant, you have to explain your decision not to have amnio, justify yourself. If you don't use prenatal screening and have a child with a disability that could have been detected, a child that could have been aborted, then is it your own fault?

As health becomes more and more of a national obsession, I wonder what lengths we will go to to have healthy children. I read an ad not long ago in the UCLA student newspaper, under the bold-face heading, "SPERM DONORS." "Financially secure couple (husband sterile following injury) wish to have two children and hope to find three donors who are close matches to each other. . . . those interested should be Caucasian; at least 5 ft. 10 in; fair (without freckles), and with blue eyes. . . . Generally this family enjoys long lives and retains good teeth, sight and hearing into old age. They do not appear to suffer with the common complaints of age such as arthritis, heart disease, senility or strokes. All the men keep their hair."

There was a list of fees to be paid—twenty-five dollars for each semen service; five hundred dollars "following Amniotic Analysis and establishment of a satisfactory pregnancy at the 16th week (3 donors) each. (If the tests are UNsatisfactory, this pregnancy will be terminated and 'repeat' services will be required from the same Donors.)"

I suppose the couple who placed that ad figures as long as you're going to use a sperm donor, why not go for the best? Why not try and find one from a family that not only doesn't have genetic illnesses but keeps hair and teeth, and doesn't suffer from heart disease or arthritis. But what happens to people who are that concerned with having a healthy child if their child gets hit by a car or maybe isn't that smart or is frail and sickly? Assuming such efforts at selecting for health were successful (a big assumption) what would it be like for that person to go through life never being sick? A man or woman of steel, a body impervious to disease, never facing those deaths of the old physical self that are a sort of skin-shedding.

I think too about how at one point during the meeting Rayna asked Adrienne and me if our mothers had worked when we were children; and how she'd seemed surprised when I said yes. It's part of the stereotype, that disabled children always require so much care, that our mothers can't live their own lives. But there can be a grain of truth in stereotypes: it's true that when there is extra work, because of illness, a disability, it's almost always the mother who does it. Yet we could link our struggles for women, for disabled people, working together for better social services, disability rights legislation, working for more equitable distribution of work within families, instead of seeing our interests as unalterably opposed.

*

The things that we talked about at Barnard, they really are the easy things, easy compared to in vitro fertilization and embryo transfer – high technology means for helping infertile women to become pregnant – and genetic engineering – the possibility that in the near future scientists will be able to change "defective" genes.

Thinking about reproductive technology is hard for feminists: it's one of those issues that doesn't just divide the movement, but divides people within themselves. If we believe in the right of women *not* to have children, then do we also have to support the right of women *to* have children? To have access to technology that will help them to do that? What about the fact that the unequal distribution of resources within our society often means that middle-class women will have sophisticated medical techniques available to them, while poor women will struggle to get basic medical care? Can we get access to these technologies without increasing medical domination over women's bodies? Do these hamper our finding new ways for adults and children to have real connections beyond biological parenting and outside of the nuclear family? What about the very real pain that infertile women feel? Do we think about control of our bodies only in terms of freedom from state control, or do we also think of it in ways that are more active?

In the newspaper recently there was a story about orphaned embryos frozen in Australia; the embryos belonged to a rich, childless American couple who were killed in a plane crash. There are ethical issues about what to do with the embryos: Are they living entities (things? people?)? Do they have rights? Do they have the right to be implanted in someone else? And there is the legal question: are they heirs to the couple's fortune?

At first glance, you would think, this one's easy: if you believe in abortion rights, then you say those embryos aren't living. They are a mass of cells, protoplasm, genetic potential. But for me, the argument for abortion rights is not so much an argument about when life begins as it is about women's rights to control our bodies. There is an enormous difference between a woman having an abortion – an experience that will stay with her for the rest of her life – and a doctor casually flushing embryos down a hospital sluice.

Reproductive technology is developed first of all for animals – usually cattle, because of the Western world's appetite for dairy products and beef. Anything that can be done to cattle can be done to (or, depending on your point of view, for) humans. There is embryo transfer. The genetically desirable cow is "superovulated" – given a drug which makes her produce many eggs. The ova are then removed and fertilized with frozen sperm from a prize bull. The embryos are then implanted in female rabbits, which are shipped to various genetically less desirable cows. The rabbits are then "sacrificed," the embryo is removed and implanted in the surrogate mother-cow.

This same technology is possible for women. Thus, a woman who doesn't want stretch marks or a woman with a heart condition can hire someone else to bear a child for her. Just as we can hire someone to clean our house or to cook our dinner for us, we can hire someone to bear our children for us. Just as we can find ourselves forced to type someone else's novel when we would rather be writing our own, we could find ourselves bearing children for another woman, saving up so we can have one of our own or go to grad school or make the down payment on a house.

Before an embryo is implanted, the genetic material of that embryo can be examined, and decisions about whether or not to implant it in a woman's uterus can be made on the basis of what that examination reveals. You can tell if the embryo is going to develop Down's Syndrome, for instance.

Certain genotypes are more susceptible to some environmental pollutants than others. Thus, you might be able to say that a certain embryo's genetic structure revealed that it would probably develop respiratory problems in response to current levels of air pollution. Thus, the disability of asthma in response to environmental toxicity could be prevented – through getting rid of those who were sensitive to air pollution.

And soon genetic engineering will make it possible to change the genes that cause some genetic diseases. Of course, you then have to decide what's a defective gene and what isn't.

It will even be possible, before too long, to introduce human genes into primates, creating a race of sub-humans. The fantasies of racists would become realities. In this brave new world, there would be no need for the Neo-Pavlovian Conditioning Rooms of Aldous Huxley's novel. The Betas would not have to listen to speakers which droned: "'Alpha children wear grey. They work much harder than we do, because they're so frightfully clever. I'm really awfully glad I'm a Beta, because I don't work so hard. And then we are much better than the Gammas and the Deltas. Gammas are stupid. . . . '" It would be right there, in their genes.

I close my eyes and lean my face against the stiff fabric of the airplane seat. I imagine a world where the air is thick and grey – although there are magnificent sunsets, because of all the pollutants in the air – and embryos are routinely flushed from wombs and tested to be sure that they are resistant to radiation and toxicity – that is, that they do not have what has come to be known as the sicknesses of "radiation sensitivity" or "toxicity intolerance."

The working class becomes the working race: drones who are half-human, half-primate carry out the routine tasks of the world.

Maybe it would be better if the world just got blown up. I'll take the bang, not the whimper.

Someone shakes my shoulder and says, "We're about to land. You need to put your seat belt on."

I walk into the terminal with my head fuzzy from sleeping on the airplane and spinning a little too.

TWO

7

When I was pregnant – pregnant for the second time, pregnant and expecting a baby – I became a pure vessel in a toxic sea. I didn't pump my own gas, I didn't eat liver – liver is the body's toxic waste dump. The book says, "Remember that pregnancy is a normal, healthy state." But it also says, don't take a hot tub, avoid heavy traffic, don't go swimming in polluted water. Stay away from cigarette smoke, don't clean the oven. Don't chew sugarless gum. Stay away from food additives. Bottled water is probably a good idea. Pregnancy is a normal state; the world's just out of kilter.

A friend of mine said, "It is not true that women are controlled by their hormones" and she dropped her voice to a whisper " – except when we're pregnant." My first trimester, I lived in a world of constant queasiness, exhaustion and keen emotion. My feelings were so heightened that when I sat down to write, I was with my characters in an instant, crying with them, laughing with them.

But I was so homesick for San Francisco. Mark is an actor, and we had moved from San Francisco to L.A. a few months before for his career. I was still commuting up to San Francisco every week to teach a writing workshop. Every trip home made me love San Francisco more, made it harder for me to live here.

In San Francisco, I would get ecstatic about riding on

the Muni: this was not a car, I was not isolated in my little brown box, driving past other people isolated in their little white, green, blue, yellow, red boxes. Old women trundled onto the 31 Ocean Beach, scarves tied under their chins. They wore thick coats although the day was warm. They were talking a Slavic language, and I decided they were Ukrainian, refugees from Stalin. They placed their purses right in the center of their laps and held onto them by the body, not the straps. A man who was drunk boarded the bus. He stepped slowly and gingerly, walking as if he were quite sober but the earth was sloshed.

A woman stood on the street corner by the BART station carrying a sign that read, "When you swear, don't say God damn. Do say Devil damn. Don't say Son of a Bitch. Do say Devil Bitch."

Grace Paley says that when she needs inspiration, she rides the New York subway and eavesdrops.

In San Francisco there is graffiti, and here in L.A. there are vanity plates. On the bathroom wall at the Red Victorian movie theater in San Francisco someone had written: "Jesus is coming," and someone else wrote under it, "in your mouth." In the bathroom at the Roxie it says, "Heterosexuals and faggots – get off the planet now!" Across the street, in Cafe Picaro, it says, "The rich get the newspapers we get the bathroom walls."

L.A. is motels, savings and loans, used car lots, nail salons, Del-Mar's Precision Brakes, First Pacific Bank, U-Save Auto Parts, Kawasaki, Taco Bell, liquor stores, body shops, Union 76, Ocean Breeze Motel, Donaldson Insurance, Cycle Parts and Insurance, Jack in the Box, Golden West Meats, One Hour Metropolitan Cleaning, Nina's Pizza, a Shell Station, Nationwide Baby Shops, a Standard Station, Friendly Computers and of course sushi. And me driving past it all in my little brown box.

This city is a hundred years old but try and find some trace of its history. Every culture is swallowed up and spat out as a franchise. Taco Bell. Benihana of Tokyo. Numero Uno Pizza. Pup 'N' Taco. Kentucky Fried Chicken. Fast food sushi. Teriyaki Bowl.

Take the 10 to the 110 to the 101. Get off at the Hollywood Exit. Santa Monica Freeway to Harbor Freeway to Hollywood Freeway.

On my way to work at the clinic in Orange County, I drive past the Coppertone sign. It is automated: the puppy is pulling the little girl's bikini bottom up and down, up and down. Drive past the convention center, surely the only extant example of neo-Assyrian architecture, with squared parapets and bas-relief sculptures. O Hammurabi! O Nebuchadnezzar! I round the bend and am greeted by the world's largest American flag.

And every Saturday morning at the abortion clinic, I said, "Hi. How are you all doing? I'm Anne . . . "

It was January of 1985; Reagan had just been inaugurated for his second term. It seemed that at least once a week there was a new abortion clinic being gutted by fire or bombed. The media was full of talk of terrorism, but these clinic bombings did not count as terrorism. Terrorism meant plots that were being hatched by dark-eyed foreigners; terrorism meant Third World fanatics and threats to our American way of life; it meant something too terrible to be imagined that hadn't happened yet. It didn't mean the bombs that were going off all around us.

It wasn't so bad that the head of the FBI was saying that violence against abortion clinics wasn't terrorism; I expected that of him. But why wasn't there any popular outrage about these bombings? Why weren't women marching? Where were the one million women who had safe abortions each year? Why weren't they in the streets? Why weren't they just saying to their families and the people they work with and their friends: I had an abortion. Where was the women's movement?

Linda, a co-worker, came up to me in the hallway and said, "Come in the sterile room. There's a twelve-week fetus that came through nearly whole. It's neat."

Shock. That was the only thing I felt. I can't—I don't want to—and Linda is a midwife.

"This is called confronting your fears," I said.

It was absolutely white, a two-inch polliwog with miniature fingers and toes. I breathed out, relieved at how not-human it looked.

Sometimes I loved working at the clinic: I felt like a miracle worker. Women came in and their futures were transformed. I was of use, and I thought how rare that was in this world: to get paid for doing something worth doing; to meet a need that wasn't manufactured on Madison Avenue or Wall Street, a need that wasn't born of self-hatred.

But, sometimes I hated it. I hated to see women in pain. The pain never lasted for very long—a minute maybe—but still it was probably the most painful thing they'd ever felt. I hated to hear women say:

"I just killed my baby."

"I'm never going to have sex again."

A few women told me, when it was over, that they understood how the "right to life" felt, or that abortion shouldn't be legal. (Save me from my power, save me from control over my life. Give me a father-state to tell me what I must do and can't do. Give me answers cast in stone.)

Two women who are roughly my mother's age read an earlier version of this book: one of them says, "An abortion clinic! That sounds like heaven on earth." They tell me stories about being blindfolded, and then driven around and around in the backs of cars with strange men, the name and phone number from a friend of a friend.

"My second abortion?" one of them says. "I can't talk about it. It was the worst experience of my life."

I wonder what happened? Was she raped? That happened sometimes, the abortionist forcing women to have sex with him before he operated. Did an instrument pierce her womb? Did she get an infection? Was she scared to go for help? Did she go for help and did the nurses and doctors have to stand by and watch and wait for her to pass a piece of fetal tissue in the blood gushing from her; scared that if they acted before then, they could be charged with performing an illegal abortion?

Each victory sets the stage for the next round of struggle.

I was sitting in the kitchen of the clinic, talking with another co-worker, Ginny. I had heard that her first baby died, and wanted to ask her about it. Wondering if I should or not. I let the words tumble out of my mouth:

"Ginny, how did you lose your first baby?–Do you mind talking about this?"

"No. I don't mind. She was a stillbirth. She was breech, and so we went into the hospital, Kaiser. The fetal monitor was broken and so when she went into distress they didn't know it. . .

"With that pregnancy, my first pregnancy, I did everything I was supposed to do, everything. I took thirty vitamins a day, and followed the Brewer diet. The second time, I did what I felt like doing–"

The sight of Ginny, sitting there picking at her Mexican food as I was picking at mine, was a comfort. Losing a baby is terrible, but not the worst. The worst would be dying yourself. You can go on. People do go on.

*

Another Saturday, and I was so groggy with first trimester tiredness. "OK. Have I taken everybody's blood pressure – except your's, Carol, I'll get to you after I do the explanation.... The doctor'll be here in a few minutes. I'm going to go over the abortion procedure with you, and answer any questions that you have, or talk about anything you need to talk about... "

When I finished, one woman said, "I'm fourteen weeks pregnant. Is it the same for me?"

"Pretty much. You have to sign a different consent form... The cannula will be larger, and you'll probably need to be dilated more." Shit. I really didn't want to see a late abortion, not now. Not at this stage in my pregnancy.

Constance called me out of the room. "That's a fake abortion. The woman who's fourteen weeks."

"Huh?"

"She doesn't want an abortion. Her boyfriend dragged her here. He's waiting outside."

Back in the room, I touched the woman's arm and said, "Constance explained your situation to me."

An hour later, she was lying in the recovery room, a hot water bottle pressed against her abdomen, as if she has had the abortion he tried to make her have. Her boyfriend was there. He thought she'd had an abortion. I wondered what would happen to her when he found out the truth.

"Feeling better?" I asked.

"Yes," she said, and smiled.

A woman came to the clinic. I was trying to talk to her through an opening in the supposedly bulletproof plexiglass. She was asking me what happened to the fetus after the abortion. I was a little suspicious of her: was she an anti-abortionist?

"Are you pregnant?" I asked, looking straight at her.

"Yes," she said.

"Just a second," I said. "I'll let you in." I came around and unlocked the door and brought her back into the reception room.

"You see," she said, "because of my religious beliefs, I want to make sure that the fetus is buried, not cremated." Her eyes welled with tears.

"Are you sure that you want to have an abortion?"

"No, I don't want to. But my boyfriend's going to leave me if I don't, and I already have one child, I just wouldn't be able to make it without him."

"Are you sure this is what you want?" I say. No, stupid, she just told you she doesn't want to have an abortion.

"I've been to counseling with my boyfriend, at Planned Parenthood, he just won't–"

She had come to us because no one else would help her see about getting her fetus buried.

Every day at the clinic I confronted what it meant to have some control over our wombs and less control over our social circumstances. You can decide to no longer be pregnant, you can walk into a clinic and plunk down your Medi-Cal card, if you're lucky enough to live in a state that still provides government funding, or two hundred dollars in cash, but you can't decide not to be poor anymore, or to have support so that you can finish school, or to have a partner who wants to raise a child with you.

It's ironic: twenty years ago, the women's movement started talking about the right of women to control our reproductive lives: our right to birth control, to abortion. We've won the right, however tenuously, but now control of reproduction is expected: we are expected to have children when we can afford them, to schedule our pregnancies to coincide with the demands of the world of education and employment. A hundred years ago, my great-grandmother left instructions for what to do in the event of her death or the death of both herself and her child.

Now, we don't just expect the births of our children to be joyful occasions, we expect to have children when we want them; we expect them to be healthy.

Our victories are always partial ones: we win part of what we wanted and then find our victories turned into something else.

Years later, I will read a quote from the nineteenth century socialist and artist, William Morris: "[Women] fight and lose the battle, and the thing they fought for comes about in spite of their defeat, and when it comes turns out not to be what they meant, and other [women] have to fight for what they meant under another name."

I am walking out the back door, and I see a plastic jar of tissue and blood waiting to be sent to the path lab; and in the plastic jar a tiny perfect white hand, it looks like the hand of a not very realistic doll. Anti-abortion propaganda often shows just a hand or just a foot, because feet and hands develop so much earlier than everything else. The hand looks human, while the heart is still a primitive thump, the brain no bigger than a pea, the whole a white jelly-thing. But it's close, too close not to trouble me.

That flat palm reaching up through a wine-red wash of blood. Why does that stay with me? Surely it isn't looking human that makes us human.

Would I have asked myself these questions ten, twelve years ago? Would they have been doubts that niggled at the edge of my mind, never forming into words? Is it the current political climate that does this?

A few months later, back in San Francisco, I went to another meeting of the Committee to Defend Reproductive Rights. We watched a video, "Silent Scream," purporting to show the scream of a fetus being aborted. Then we talked: about the shift in emphasis from the woman to the embryo/fetus; do we address people's questions about when life begins or does that mean letting the Right set the terms of the debate; how do we talk about the ethics of abortion?

Another disabled woman had joined CDRR. She is blind and has cerebral palsy. In CDRR, everyone raises their hands and waits for the chair to call on them before they speak. Except for Jaime, who kept talking out of turn, and no one would tell her to raise her hand and wait till she got called on, like they would with anyone else. And I thought: "Fucking liberals."

And then someone said that life is socially defined, and that the biological definitions of life are not the ultimate ones. When we have this sort of broad-ranging discussion in CDRR, we write with felt tip markers on butcher paper the boiled-down essence of what we're saying. It's a way of holding together all the disparate views, making sure that ideas don't get lost in the shuffle.

And so someone wrote in blue felt tip: "Life does not equal the right to live."

Oh, great, I thought. Life is socially defined. Now, who gets to make the definitions and who gets defined out of existence? Disabled people? Jews? Old people?

I wanted to say something then, but I didn't. Because I didn't want to sound like a crank, like a woman with a one-track mind. Because I didn't want to get accused of calling people Nazis.

About that same time, I read an article in *Ms.* on anti-abortion terrorism. It said: "Joseph Scheidler [a leader of the movement to disrupt abortion clinics] and the extremists claim that abortion is the American holocaust, the equivalent of the Nazi Holocaust. The irony is that Hitler was antichoice: he outlawed abortion in Nazi Germany and one of the key goals of the Third Reich was to force Aryan women to have as many children as possible."

I wrote a letter saying that's only partly true. Abortion was illegal but widely tolerated during the pre-Nazi period of the Weimar Republic. And while the majority of women found abortions impossible to obtain in the Nazi period, Hitler did legalize abortion for women who were carrying fetuses believed to be "defective" – almost always women who were themselves disabled or who had a disabled family member. These women were often forced to have abortions.

One researcher who studied deaf survivors of the Nazi era reported that most of those who underwent abortion were past their fifth month. Obviously, those women who were "defectives" or married to "defectives" tried to hide their pregnancies.

I try to see the faces behind that statistic. I see a deaf woman sitting in a frayed overstuffed chair, crying, her make-up running down her face, in a third floor flat, waiting for the policeman coming up the stairs, her hand pressed against her belly to feel the last kicks of what should have been her child. Who turned her in: the worker at the deaf social club? Her resentful sister who had just joined the Nazi Party?

Sister, we who should remember you have written your memories out of our history.

How do I put these things together? These random facts, not so random:

Nearly eighty percent of all people in the U.S. support abortion in the case of (unspecified) "fetal defect."

When you are pregnant, suddenly everyone is asking you: "How old are you?" (i.e., Are you over thirty-five?)

That health has become the overriding metaphor for what is good in our society. If women have doubts about whether or not they did the right thing in having an abortion, they'll often tell you they had an abortion because they were worried about their health, or about their future child's health.

That the Nazis drew tremendous metaphoric power from their claim to be creating the *heilanstaat*, the healthy state. The healthy body and the healthy state became one.

58

Genocide began as a cleansing of the defective, disease-ridden dregs.

If abortion is acceptable because a fetus's brain isn't fully developed, and therefore they aren't human, then what is a person with brain damage? Even though I base my beliefs about abortion on *women*'s rights and status, not on that of the fetus within her, plenty of people don't.

I like living in hard places. Well, I'm not so sure I like it: I just seem to find myself there a lot.

8

It was one in the afternoon. I'd been at the clinic since seven that morning.

"Constance, can I take my break?" A question that was sure to elicit one of two answers: how can I possibly be asking to take my break when we are so impossibly, impossibly busy or what do I mean I haven't had my break yet, I should have asked for it a long time ago, she didn't realize...

I got the latter of the answers and I went downstairs to the health food store. It was the kind of health food store where everything was wrapped in plastic or cellophane. There were thirty- or forty-year-old framed autographed pictures of Cary Grant and Bing Crosby on the wall. Five stools sat before a counter in the back. On the wall were white paper placemats that had been written on with blue felt tip pen. "Try our PROTEIN POWER SUPREME: Milk, banana, wheat germ, protein powder and honey!" Along one side, it said "WOW!" and along the other "DELICIOUS!" Both were inside the kind of jagged shapes that surround the words "POW" or "SHAZZAM" in comic books. I ordered a fresh squeezed orange juice and a bran muffin, even though I knew the muffin had so much honey I wouldn't be able to finish it.

I had been reading a book about diet during pregnancy which preached the Brewer diet—one woman I knew

called it "the football team diet," because you're supposed to eat enough food to feed a football team. The
book warned: your baby is growing at an amazingly fast
rate—in fact, if we grew throughout our lives at the same
rate as we do in the womb, each of us would weigh two
trillion times as much as the earth does. If you skip a single
meal, you are jeopardizing your baby's well-being. Eat
whenever you are hungry as much as you want. I *like* being
pregnant, I decided. I took back a container of low fat raspberry yogurt, and, after a minute or so of consideration, a
Jack LaLanne Protein Bar.

I sat in the staff lounge, eating my raspberry yogurt,
talking with Linda. One of the posters hanging on the wall
advertised a talk that Linda did at the Cambridge YWCA a
decade ago. I remembered ten years ago sitting on the
floor of the Women's Center in Cambridge (we were always sitting on the floor then—sitting in a chair seemed almost reactionary) while a woman was holding up that
same poster and talking about a midwife from California
who was coming to talk at the Cambridge Y. Linda was
something of a legend, having been arrested in the early
seventies in Santa Cruz for practicing medicine without a
license.

She asked me if I was planning a home birth. I said,
yes, and asked her what she knew about the L.A. Childbirth Center.

"They're pretty good. They can be a little snooty
sometimes."

"Snooty?"

"Too professional. They might give you a hard time
about your having one leg shorter than the other... "

"It's a little more complicated than that," I said.

This is my fate, I think, to be caught between doctors
who think my body is a wreck and want to slice me open
and try vainly to make me "normal" and alternative
health people who think that there's nothing wrong with
me that a little brown rice and meditation won't cure.

*

It was reading Barbara Katz Rothman's book, *Giving Birth: Alternatives in Childbirth* that had convinced me to have a home birth, an idea I'd previously considered quite nutty.

I knew that some of my parents' friends had been born at home and it seemed like a quaint custom from the past. But when I lived in England at the age of eighteen, a med student friend casually mentioned having accompanied a midwife to a home birth, the baby having plopped into the world on a bedding of the scandal sheet, *The News of the World*. At home? How could that be? It seemed almost impossible, bordering on the medieval.

Faith, my best friend from high school, gave birth in the early seventies in a log cabin in Vermont during a blizzard, with only her twenty-year-old boyfriend in attendance. She'd taken Lamaze classes, and afterwards reported with some astonishment to my mother, "Mrs. Finger, it *hurt*." The fact that Faith held her baby almost constantly and refused to have Amla (she was named after the first sounds she made) vaccinated confirmed my belief that home birth was for people who had been carried somewhat too far by the wild currents of the sixties.

I was skeptical enough that when I read an article in *Ms.* that reported that midwives had lower infant and maternal mortality rates than obstetricians – even under difficult circumstances – I simply refused to believe it. High tech medicine could "do" more than low tech (or no tech) medicine. It had to be better.

True, I didn't like doctors or hospitals much at all, but I liked most "alternative" health people I ran into even less. I'd been to too many parties where an ardent devotee of natural health had engaged me in a conversation and casually, oh so casually, brought up the wonders worked by her chiropractor/naturopath/herbalist. Would I like his number? (A blind friend of mine, when she gets approached with these offers, says in an absolutely puzzled and sincere tone of voice, "What for?")

I usually was polite, took the phone numbers, and threw them out when I got home. It was easier than trying to convince someone that my nerves were dead and that my muscles had atrophied decades ago, and bringing dead muscles and nerves back was about as easy as raising a body from the grave. If I tried that, my rescuer would usually smile and tell me (a) about someone a friend of hers knew who had cured himself of cancer through visualization; (b) about a mountain community in Afghanistan where people ate only goat's milk yogurt and dandelion leaves and where everyone lived to be 150, at which time they expired in their sleep with profoundly wise expressions on their faces; or (c) that all my ills, including my desire not to be healthy, were due to karma and if I didn't work it out in this life, there was always the next one.

But what troubled me most about the alternative health movement was its tendency to seek the quick fix. The new herb and the latest meditation technique are greeted with all the fanfare formerly reserved for medical breakthroughs. Health becomes an elusive commodity sought through visits to health spas, accupuncturists, psychotherapists, homeopaths, chiropractors, nutritionists, herbalists, naturopaths. As in Western medicine, disease and death are enemies to be battled, albeit with different weapons.

Whenever I am sick I reread Virginia Woolf's essay "On Being Ill." Woolf writes of "the wastes and deserts of the soul a slight attack of influenza brings to view, what precipices and lawns sprinkled with bright flowers a little rise of temperature reveals... how we go down into the pit of death and feel the waters of annihilation close above our heads and wake thinking to find ourselves in the presence of angels and the harpers when we have a tooth out and come to the surface in the dentist's arm-chair and confuse his 'Rinse the mouth – rinse the mouth' with the greeting of the Deity stooping from the floor of Heaven to welcome us... " It reminds me that illness can be experienced, rather than fought against.

The notion of taking responsibility for one's own health too often slides into a blaming the victim stance. We end up seeking piecemeal, individualized solutions to complex social problems. We swallow our vitamins, worry about the link between aluminum and Alzheimer's disease, and the radiation given off by luminous dial clocks, while this country produces over 200 million tons of toxic waste every year, there are enough nuclear weapons to wipe out the earth several times over, and twenty million people could live for a year on the grain used by the U.S. beer and liquor industry annually. In New York City, nearly half of all children who die before the age of one are from families so poor they cannot even afford funerals, and so they are buried in mass graves in Potter's Field.

And yet, at the same time, I had to confront what my own experience of hospitals and medicine had been. The memories of my first hospitalization, when I had polio shortly before my third birthday, are fuzzy. But beginning at the age of six, I returned to hospitals again and again for surgery.

The walls of the hospitals were always painted those same pastels that schoolroom walls were painted in the fifties: unnatural lime greens, pale yellows and tans. Someone once told me that the theory was that those colors were calming: bright colors would cause emotional turmoil.

The nurses all wore uniforms that outdid the military in their attention to rank and detail. Their shoes were white, their stockings were white, their starched uniforms were white, as were the caps that were bobby-pinned to their hair. The caps showed what nursing school they had gone to as a nun's wimple reveals her order.

The first time I had surgery, I was six years old. I had been prepared for my trip to the hospital with a child's book about a boy – was he really named Timmy? – who had his tonsils out. "When Timmy woke up, his throat was very sore. The nurse brought him strawberry ice cream, his favorite flavor, and he felt better right away!" Grimm's Fairy Tales, with their worlds of inexplicable evil, would have been more appropriate.

I was admitted the day before surgery. My mother was allowed to accompany me to the room, and to stay with me for a few minutes. It was made clear that an exception was being made since it was not visiting hours, which were from three to four in the afternoon and seven to eight at night. She went down to the waiting area and I cried until she returned at three.

After dinner, a nurse came in and laid a rubber sheet across the middle of the white-sheeted bed. I was laid face down across it. I could hear metal clanking against metal, a packet being ripped open, something sloshing in a bowl. I wanted to know what was going on, but I was afraid to look at the tray of instruments. I heard the sound of water being sucked into a bulb syringe; the smell of vaseline and soapy water.

A nozzle entered my anus; I could feel the soapy water being squeezed into my rectum; and then the lather working at my guts. I was told to sit on the stainless steel bedpan. A few minutes later, I heard strange rumblings coming from within me, followed by noises that filled me with shame: belches and loud, uncontrollable farts that repeated and repeated. The nurse left the room. Liquid shit poured from me. My stomach cramped. Every time I thought that it was finished, it would start again. The room was filled with the stink of shit and soap. It went on and on and on.

I was deeply ashamed. I was lonely and frightened, and

yet I was glad I had been left alone. I was a baby again, a baby who could not control her own shit, a baby who just went and went and went. Finally it was over. The nurse retrieved the bedpan. The lights were turned out and I went to sleep.

I was awakened the next morning at the standard time of quarter to six with the lights in my room suddenly being flicked on, a hand shaking my shoulder, and a thermometer popped into my mouth. Two fingers on my wrist took my pulse. An hour later, I heard the sound of rubber wheels against the linoleum floor, the clanking of the breakfast trays. I was hungry, my throat was dry, but I knew that I could have nothing to eat.

Alone, in my room, I pretended to be asleep. I kept on pretending to be asleep as I was lifted onto a gurney and wheeled down the corridor, down an elevator, and down another long corridor. Finally, I let my eyes flutter open: we were moving down a dark basement corridor, with pipes painted an institutional pinkish-beige overhead and strange metal fittings jutting out from the walls. I closed my eyes immediately, determined to continue with my pretense of sleep.

Again, I was being transferred: from the gurney which had become warm with the heat of my sweating body onto a cold metal table. Two straps were fastened across me. I opened my eyes. The image in my mind is distinct. The room was tiled in blue. On the wall opposite were long shelves, with row upon row of glass jars with thick glass stoppers.

I looked above me: there was the brightest lamp I had ever seen in my life, with ten or twenty bulbs set into one fixture. It reminded me of the eye of the bumblebee that had been shown in close-up on *The Wonderful World of Disney*, the hexagons coming together to form one gigantic, frightening goggle-eye.

I am asleep, I am asleep, I am asleep. No one touches me. I lie there strapped against the narrow metal table.

I wonder, looking back, at the way the nurses who moved around me seemed to accept the fact that I was a-sleep. Like most six-year-olds faking sleep I probably shut my eyes too tightly; certainly, I must not have made my body a dead weight as I was moved from the bed to the gurney, the gurney to the operating table. Yet no one spoke to me, no one held my hand.

Suddenly, the room was filled with people. A black tri-angular mask was put over my mouth and nose. The fumes from the ether were so strong that as I breathed it in, I could taste it in the back of my mouth. I struggled for air, but the more deeply I breathed the more overpowering the sense of being suffocated became. I forgot that at all costs I must pretend to be asleep. I opened my eyes, only to discover that the blackness of the mask was everywhere: I could no longer see. I was spinning downwards, swirling wildly out of control, down into some darkness and I tried to stop but I could not.

When I woke up my mother was there, as I had been promised. What I had not been told was that she would have four heads. Still, it was a comfort to see those four heads bending in unison towards me, and to hear her four mouths say my name.

I closed my eyes and fell back down into unconscious-ness. When I opened them again, her three extra heads had disappeared; instead she had a row of perhaps twenty mouths, stretching from her chin up to her forehead; her twenty red-red lips moved in together. I begged her not to make me have another operation; I told her I would give her a hundred dollars, I told her I would do anything, only please, please, please not to make me have surgery again.

I had five more operations. I didn't walk any better af-ter all of them than I had before. Yet the surgeon had done a "beautiful job," I heard often. The scars were psycholo-gical, but they were literal, too. Dr. Friedman, who was such a good surgeon, didn't seem to care about how I looked. He used seven clumsy stitches to suture up a five inch long incision. My left leg is covered with seven thick fat ugly scars. It was as if he wrote on my body: "Ugly. Piece of junk. Ruined. Doesn't matter."

Years later, I tried to describe my experience as a hospitalized child to my therapist. She was a warm woman, usually quite empathetic, and, as the psychological jargon has it, "non-directive." I was talking about the real terror that I had felt as a six-year-old child having surgery.

She cut me off with, "But you were asleep."

I tried to tell her that that was what I had been led to expect; but that in fact, being put under with ether was nothing like falling asleep.

"You were asleep," she repeated.

I wonder if she was the daughter of a doctor, or the wife of one. Perhaps. At any rate, there was something inside her so powerful that it made her forget all of her good therapeutic techniques. Instead she became a wall: you did not feel anything. It did not hurt.

After all, they tried. They were doing the best they could. It's a given: that what was done to us was for our own good; and that the horrors of the past have been swept away by scientific medicine.

Despite my experience in hospitals, I had never considered having anything other than a hospital birth. But Barbara's book made a convincing case for home birth being as safe, or safer, than hospital birth.

True, there's more technology available in a hospital. But that very technology can cause its own set of problems. Virtually all women giving birth in hospitals now are hooked up to an electric fetal monitor, a machine which charts the fetal heart rate and the strength of the laboring woman's contractions. The problems with fetal heart monitors are legion. Sometimes they misread the fetal heart rate, doubling or halving it. Sometimes they pick up the mother's heart rate instead of the baby's, leading to the mistaken conclusion that the fetus is experiencing distress.

Even a perfectly functioning fetal monitor has problems. One of the concerns is that an external fetal monitor uses ultrasound to pick up the baby's heartbeat. The long term effects of exposure to ultrasound are unknown, although some studies link it to cellular changes. But the main problem with fetal monitors is that they frequently give false positive readings – they indicate fetal distress when in fact none exists, and increase the rate of Cesareans. The monitor also makes it difficult for a woman to move about freely, which can prolong labor and make it more painful.

A climate of fear and dehumanization is created by the presence of a beeping metal box, flashing out the fetal heart rate second by second. Because obstetricians see body and mind as separate, they ignore the effect on the laboring woman of these procedures. When an animal in labor is in the presence of danger, her labor will sometimes stop and resume when she feels herself to be safe again. Fear can slow and stop labor.

But in the hospital, if a woman's labor slows down or stops or if it is not deemed to be proceeding quickly enough according to a predetermined curve of what a normal labor should look like – then the woman is often given pitocin to speed up her labor. Like many obstetrical interventions, pitocin is becoming routine. Many women find a fast labor more difficult than a slow one. Women also say that the contractions caused by pitocin are particularly difficult to deal with – solid pain rather than the peaks and valleys of unaugmented labor. One intervention almost inexorably leads to the next: the "beached whale" position necessary for the monitor to work slows down labor, which is then augmented with pitocin. The pitocin makes labor more painful, so the woman may need painkillers or even local anesthesia to help her manage the pain of the labor. Painkillers can slow down labor and contribute to fetal distress, as can local anesthesia. The administration of local anesthesia requires a number of interlocking interventions: an IV in one arm; a blood pressure gauge attached to the other; artifical rupture of membranes, if the waters have not already broken; and a fetal monitor. Once a woman has been administered local anesthesia, she has a much higher risk of forceps delivery or Cesarean section.

By contrast, in the Netherlands, the vast majority of women give birth under the care of midwives, without drugs – simply, naturally. The C-section rate is under three percent; and their infant mortality rate is one of the lowest in the world. Their excellent mortality rate is almost certainly a result of accessible health care and social services. Yet this statistic also disproves the notion, common in the U.S., that widespread use of high tech medicine is necessary to save the lives and health of mothers and babies.

There are two contradictory tendencies at work in childbirth in the U.S. One is that an increasing number of women want natural childbirth, and enter hospitals expecting to have their children in home-like alternative birth centers. The other is that the C-section rate is rising precipitiously – the national average is now twenty-one percent, and at some hospitals it is as high as forty percent for first-time mothers. Only three percent of women actually have unmedicated births.

I figured that as a disabled woman, I was a prime candidate for a Cesarean. And having a "vaginal" birth rather than an "abdominal" one was tremendously important to me. I wanted to do something that was physically courageous. A voice in my head says, say it all, even the nasty, competitive things that good socialist feminists aren't supposed to say: I wanted to do something most other women couldn't do. That wasn't the strongest reason, but that was a reason.

I wanted to give birth.

When I imagined a hospital birth, I imagined a repeat of my previous experiences in the hospital. Even short of a C-section, it was my nightmare:

You cannot see the woman. You know she is there because of the figures gathered around the table. They are masked and gowned. If you shift position, you can see her. Well, not really her, her feet in the air. Not actually her feet, their outline under the blue drape which covers them. Somewhere, far away, is her head, separated from the rest of her body by gowns and drapes. The view the doctor sees could be from a stark porno magazine: a detached cunt.

He tells the woman to push. She cannot feel the contraction; she has had an epidural and her body is numb from the belly to the knees. Her hands, her feet, her head, her shoulders, her chest are all fully awake. She can feel everything except her baby being born.

The room smells of alcohol. The woman is told to push. She has never pushed a baby out before, and since she cannot feel what she is doing, she is not quite sure she is doing it right.

"Good," the doctor says.

She feels relieved; he has told her that she is doing a good job.

The woman is tired. She is hungry and thirsty. She has not eaten since the day before, when she felt the first signs of labor. Since coming to the hospital, she has had only ice chips to suck on. Her stomach and bladder need to be empty, in case she needs a C-section.

She wonders if the nurse has had a child. The nurse is warm but still the woman hesitates to ask her. It seems too personal a question.

In the book that she read, there was a list of nearly forty questions that one was supposed to ask a prospective doctor. How many births have you attended? What percentage of your patients walk around during labor? What percentage of your patients have Cesareans? What percentage of your patients need episiotomies?

At her second visit, she started asking him the questions. He smiled fondly at her. She felt slightly foolish. He used a few words that she did not know. He told her that if she wants to have a drug-free labor, he's willing to go along with that; but she shouldn't be a martyr. Most women, he tells her, need something. He asks her if she has a high pain threshold. She asks about a fetal monitor. He tells her that infant mortality rates have fallen since the introduction of the monitor. He tells her that all births have to be considered high risk until they are over.

She has grown used to the beeping of the machine, to the green numbers being flashed out on its screen. She hardly hears it anymore. She has grown used to the sight of gowned figures, to the antiseptic smell of the hospital.

She cannot feel her contraction. The machine says that she is having a contraction and the doctor tells her to push. Because she is lying flat on her back, she has to push against gravity. When the head is at what the doctor calls the outlet, he makes a slight cut, then uses low forceps to ease the baby from her body. It is held upside down for her to see. She has been delivered.

Going to my first appointment at the birth center, I felt like a supplicant. I've got a normal pelvis, would you like to see an x-ray of it? Yes, I've got asthma, but I only wheeze when I'm around cats and goose down. No, I'm not diabetic, I've never had VD. Am I low enough risk? Will you take me? Yes.

I went back once a month during the first two trimesters, seeing one of the two midwives, Laura and Vi. Laura was my age, also pregnant with her first baby, but about three months further along than I was. Vi was older, the mother of six children.

The difference between midwifery and obstetrics was apparent just in the way those routine prenatal visits were conducted. For instance, instead of handing a sample of urine to a nurse to test it, I tested my urine myself. I weighed myself too. The visits themselves were leisurely – usually half an hour – and the talk was sometimes directly focused on birth and sometimes about where we had gone for the weekend. At some point during the visit I would undress and clamber up on the table. It had always been one of the consummate mysteries of medicine to me – why the doctor could see you undressed, but not undressing. Are you eating enough? Laura always asked.

Every night I dreamt of houses. A square clapboard house on a square plot of land in Indiana, with a wrought metal fence and elm trees and a cupola on top. A rambling white house with scuffed steps and a strangely, half-tended yard. Always, the houses are old and roomy; and, although in my dreams I never see the inside, I know that there are rooms you can wander through, and nooks under the stairs; there are wooden floors that have been scuffed and polished and scuffed and polished, and in the cellars and attics, things other people have left behind.

Each Monday I flew up to San Francisco, to teach my writing workshop at the Independent Living Project. I felt at home there: I did not have to worry about being too much for these people. No one recoiled with pity when Joe said, "I have lupus. . . . They were doing a study about my family at UCSF, till the funding got cut, because four people in my family have lupus. My sister, who was the one who raised me, died of it in 1978, and her daughter died two years later. She had just turned twenty. . . . I had to learn to write all over again, after my first flare, I had lost all my memory, all my knowledge."

73

"I'm Blair. I'm psychotic. Psychotic depression. . . . Sometimes when things were very bad I would feel like a rock falling alone through outer space."

I was in a room where the struggle to write was not metaphoric, but literal: a struggle to hold a pen when aching fingers want to drop it, a fight to make hands move against cerebral palsy, a fight against fatigue. David said that since his stroke, nothing comes easy. He had to think when he drinks his coffee: put your hands around the styrofoam cup, lift it to your lips, put your lips on the cup, let your upper lip test for warmth, swallow, remove lips from cup, set cup back down, let go of cup. Like using chopsticks for the first time, but all the time, always.

We did a writing exercise in class and after five minutes I said, "OK, why don't people finish up what they're writing now." Lina said, "Anne, I've only had time to write one line."

People who aren't disabled never seem less than human to me, but they sometimes seem to be missing a dimension, glib and easy; skimmers over the surface of life, not quite as real.

In March, I flew to New York to be in a documentary film about disability. The day I left there was a picture on the front page of the *Los Angeles Times*, a late-breaking story: the Feminist Women's Health Center, the clinic where I worked, had been destroyed by fire.

I was surprised at how muted my reaction was: as if I had been half-expecting it. Even an odd sense of relief: that the thing we feared had finally happened, it was over, we didn't have to dread it anymore.

In New York, I stayed with my friend Lily, whose son Eric was eight months old.

"Look," she said, unfastening his diaper. "He's the world's only uncircumcised Jew. We just couldn't bear to have one more thing done to him—" Eric had had meconium aspiration: he had breathed in fetal stool before birth, and had spent the first week of his life in a special care unit, on oxygen, with an intravenous line running into his scalp. There was a picture of him on the wall of Lily's and Isaac's bedroom, a few weeks old, fetal still, lying on his belly with his legs drawn up, his shock of black downy hair shaved on one side.

9

And then, my second trimester began. I went from having to get up to go to the bathroom four or five times a night to sleeping through the night. Sleeping through the night – it was wonderful! My nausea disappeared. For two months I swaggered around saying, "Oh, I love being pregnant." It was true; and I'd never been healthier in my life.

It was good too to feel that bond with other women who were pregnant or had given birth; and a growing closeness with my own mother. Friends had told me it would happen, that wordless joining born of shared experience.

I'd sent my mother Barbara Katz Rothman's book about home birth. She was planning on coming here for the birth – as long as I went into labor before the school year started.

"They wouldn't fire you for taking time off, you know."

"I know," she said. "I just don't feel right about it."

"How many days have you missed in twenty years?"

"A few."

My mother told me that when my oldest sister was born she'd had a standard birth of that period, induction and full anesthesia. My sister, who weighed under five pounds at birth, had narrowly escaped being in an incubator.

"I didn't like that much," my mother said. "So I went to the library and took out Grantly Dick-Read's *Childbirth Without Fear*. Have you read that – it's pretty florid and Victorian in parts. But I did the exercises. My doctor didn't think much of it but he said that if that was what I wanted to do it was OK. After that I had all of you naturally."

I think of my mother, how brave she was, laboring without drugs but also without any companionship; in those hospital wards, strapped to a table, alone, while other laboring women, lost in the state called "twilight sleep," caused by a drug that didn't prevent pain, just made you forget it; while those other laboring women screamed and nurses with white uniforms and squeaky shoes came into her room with fat syringes and snorted, "Well, if you want to suffer, that's all right with me." I think of my slightly cynical mother reading Grantly Dick-Read who describes the phases of labor as proceeding from Elation to Relaxation and on to Exaltation. She took what she could from that, and she can remember the way the light looked coming in the window the moment I was born.

I want her so much to be with me when my baby is born.

My first taste of what being disabled and pregnant was going to be like happened in San Francisco, where I'd sublet an apartment for six weeks while I was teaching a class at San Francisco State. My roommate's puppy rushed in and out of the door as I opened it, and scampered between my legs, upsetting my fragile balance and down I tumbled, landing crying on the floor. Had I sprained my ankle, broken my toe?

I went to the emergency room at the county hospital, San Francisco General. The sign above the desk said TRIAGE NURSE. From there I was sent to Window Three.

At Window Number Three, I was directed to Window Number Two. The two men who worked at Number Two and Number Three were talking about electric batteries, earnestly, almost heatedly.

After a minute or two, the man in charge of Window Number Two said, "I need to take care of this lady."

"OK"

I started to give him my information, but his friend kept interrupting him, saying, "OK. But if you threw the battery in a tub of water, wouldn't it – " Oh, please. My foot hurts so much.

Number Two kept saying, "Let me finish this," meaning my paperwork, and Number Three said, "OK, but the positive charge is on one side, right? and the negative charge is on the other, right?"

Have a seat in the waiting area. The waiting area was filled with smoke, and I moved from seat to seat, as man after man lit up next to me.

I sat there reading my battered copy of George Orwell's *The Road to Wigan Pier*. One other person was reading a copy of *The Examiner* that was a few days old. Everyone else just sat and stared, smoking their cigarettes. Someone stubbed out a butt in the ashtray and a man across the room shuffled over and retrieved it.

"Have you got a match?" he asked me.

"Don't smoke," I said.

After an hour, my name was called and I hobbled in. There was no exam room, I had to get seen in the hallway. Take off your shoe and sock. On one side of me, a man in an orange jail jumpsuit was handcuffed with his feet chained together. On the other side, a man was sleeping. Every now and again, a doctor came over and woke up the sleeping man to ask him a question.

I was seated outside Trauma Room One. The patient

in Trauma Room One was shouting, "Fuck you. Fuck your mother. Fuck your father. Fuck your kids. Fuck everyone you know. Double-fuck your mother. Double-fuck your father..."

"What happened?" a doctor asked the man in the jail jumpsuit.

"Put my hand through a window."

From Trauma Room One: "I was mugged. I was mugged and I get brought in here and treated like I'm the criminal. You people are going to have a lawsuit on your hands. Every single one of you. None of you are ever going to practice medicine again. Not in the state of California. You fucking nurses and you fucking doctors and your fucking mothers and your fucking fathers..."

A male nurse came by and took my blood pressure. He had to take it again, because the man was yelling so loudly that he couldn't hear.

"Fuck you. Fuck every one of you. Fuck your mothers and your fathers. Fuck all your kids and fuck everyone you know..."

"Do you have a cigarette?" the prisoner handcuffed to the chair asked me.

"I'm sorry. I don't smoke."

In the end, they told me that it was probably just a broken toe, that I would be better off not having an x-ray; I got sent home with a prescription for Tylenol with codeine.

"Is it a good idea to take that when I'm pregnant?"

"Probably not."

"You fucking doctors and you fucking nurses –"

My foot turned psychedelic shades of purple and yellow and I slept with it throbbing, propped up on pillows.

Then, less than a month later, I fell again: carrying the groceries into the house, my right foot folded under me. Another emergency room, a hairline fracture. It was the hormones of pregnancy, pouring into my body, relaxing all my joints, to ease the bones of my pelvis wider. I didn't feel it at all in my unaffected joints, but in my right ankle and knee, where there were no functioning muscles to give support, I wobbled and bent. My joints were jelly, they flopped this way and that. Who else had broken bones as a side effect of pregnancy?

When I was done with my teaching, Mark flew up to San Francisco and loaded up the car for me and we drove back to Los Angeles together. Coming through the Altamont Pass, we saw a double rainbow, a good omen. I thought, things between us really are going to work out, however hard it is for me to be living in L.A. We sang songs in the car, songs he knows from growing up Pentecostal and I know from the civil rights movement.

<table>
<tr><td align="center">I sing:</td><td align="center">While he sings:</td></tr>
<tr><td align="center">This little light of mine,
I'm a gonna let it shine...
I ain't gonna let Bull
Connor put it out
I'm a gonna let it shine...</td><td align="center">This little light of mine,
I'm a gonna let it shine...
I ain't gonna let old
Satan put it out
I'm a gonna let it shine...</td></tr>
<tr><td align="center">I got the light of justice,
I'm a gonna let it shine.</td><td align="center">I got the light of Jesus,
I'm a gonna let it shine.</td></tr>
</table>

It is spring. We are moving from that awful white stucco with pink-orange trim house on Westminster to a wood house with redwood paneling and trees (well, a tree) growing in front and dogs running past – afghans, Irish setters, mutts, Golden Retrievers, a yipping miniature poodle.

It is spring. On April 20th, nearly 50,000 people marched in San Francisco; over a hundred students were arrested at Berkeley in an anti-apartheid demonstration, 2,500 demonstrated. There's hope for the world again. It is spring and we aren't all just waiting for Reagan to blow us up.

The day after I got back from San Francisco, my mother called, to tell me that her mother was in the hospital with pneumonia, they didn't think she was going to live. This was the third phone call I had gotten in the past couple of years, telling me that my grandmother was about to die. I didn't believe it.

Then around six, the phone rang and when I picked it up, there was a second's hollow silence, the way there sometimes is on a long distance call, and I knew that it was my mother calling to tell me that Grandma was dead.

I thought my pregnancy would keep her alive: that she would live to see me have her great-granddaughter. I thought that my pregnancy would not just keep her alive, but make her want to live again.

Being post-polio and pregnant was somewhat like dealing with the discomforts of pregnancy and the discomforts of old age at the same time. This must be how the biblical Sarah felt, pregnant at ninety with Isaac. I had a hiatal hernia – a bit of the stomach protrudes through my weakened diaphragm into the esophagous – common in older people and people who are post-polio. Between the growing size of my uterus and the fact that progesterone relaxes the stomach, what had been an occasional nuisance became almost the focus of my life. A constant taste of acid seared my throat. Bending over made me vomit.

Plain toast made me bilious. Orange juice was impossible. Likewise meat, any spices, anything fried – a scrambled egg in the morning made me miserable all day. My diet became limited to rice and beans (plain rice, a green pepper in the beans for flavoring), chicken, salad without dressing, cereal, homemade corn chowder, fruit, and bread eaten day after day in an unceasing round. Going out to eat was impossible. I read through recipe books, trying to find something I could eat, anything. I toted my plain chicken to dinner parties. Couldn't lie down if there was anything in my stomach, no matter how exhausted I was, because lying down made the hearthburn worse, couldn't eat anything after six p.m. so my stomach would be relatively empty when I did lie down to go to sleep.

Go a few days without using any seasonings, and you will develop a whole new understanding of European history. Those medieval overland treks to India and China in search of anise and saffron and turmeric will make perfect sense; you will understand why Christopher Columbus risked falling off the edge of the earth in pursuit of the spices of the East.

And even with all that, when I lay down at night in my bed with the head raised, raised so that gravity will keep the gastric juices in my stomach, I fought with the gastritis to stay asleep, and woke up to vomit in the middle of the night.

I collected remedies. Vi recommended papaya enzyme. Linda said that when I get up in the morning, I should drink a glass of water and then go up on my toes and bounce down – can I do that? – ten times. The force of gravity will bring your stomach down. Chew gum. Drink peppermint tea. Take two tablespoons of vinegar before you eat anything. I try everything, and most things help a little, but nothing makes me feel well, just less sick.

The fatigue was the hardest thing to deal with. I was exhausted all the time: not the exhaustion you feel after a hard day's work, but exhaustion like that of flu or depression. A slow seep.

The Feminist Women's Health Center finally reopened their clinic, but I was too exhausted to consider going back to work there.

A journal entry from that time:

How can my life feel so empty and yet it still seems as if there is no time for anything? The Women, Health and Healing conference in less than three weeks and I have no idea of what I am going to say. Call Barb and set up a time for us to go to her office.

Doldrums. I told Adrienne that I would have the rewritten version of the reproductive rights article to her in a month – that was two weeks ago – and still I haven't done a scrap of work on it. Listening to the same Bruce Springsteen tape (*Nebraska*) I have been listening to every day for the past two weeks.

Still, I am writing my five pages a day, nearly every day, and feel myself going to new places, where I have not been before. I feel as if this book has been waiting inside of me – can it really be for fourteen years – waiting for me to learn to write, waiting for me to have the experience of maternity – to come out.

I read the first chapter of it to the writing group when I was up in San Francisco, and then read it at a reading the last time I was up there. Wheeling down the aisle between the chairs at Modern Times when I was done, and a woman I don't know says to me, "That was wonderful!" (Earlier in the day I had been talking to Susan Hansel on the phone, saying I was nervous, and she said that Bob Gluck had been teaching one of her classes at State, and when she announced our reading, Bob went on about what a wonderful writer I was.) I need compliments right now, waiting to hear from New York about my book, waiting. And I kept dreaming that by this time I would have sold my paperback rights, not for anything too magnificent and wild, just for a couple of hundred thousand dollars.

I just want the phone to ring with wonderful news, that's all.

(Last night I felt her move in two places at once, and realized that one must be her hand and the other her foot. It is not a butterfly dancing in there.)

But the phone has not rung with someone telling me that my work is wonderful, Random House is interested... Instead, I am an SSI recipient, a WIC food program recipient. Coming home with my booklet of coupons – this one for five quarts of milk, this one for two dozen eggs and a pound of beans or 18 ounces of peanut butter. Mark looking sheepish while I explain to him how to use them.

"You know," I say to him, "this is the only advanced capitalist country where pregnant women don't get help from the state. In England," I say, "everyone gets help. The Queen gets free milk."

"I know," he says. "It's just that it feels like welfare."

A few nights later, we were sitting in bed and Mark said, "I still worry that I won't get enough food... I remember being hungry when I was a kid."

"When you lived with your mother or with Betty Jo?"

"Betty Jo. My mother knew how to be poor." I remember Mark's brother telling me proudly how their mother could make dinner for the whole family of eleven out of a pound of hamburger.

Another journal entry, a month later:

August 6th

Hiroshima Day.

Ten o'clock in the morning and I am just sitting down at the typewriter. My stretch marks itching, my hands itched all night. I think they were bitten by insects when we were driving through the Central Valley. I felt like the Joads when we left Los Angeles, our car kept breaking down, first a tire, stopping at busy gas station after busy gas station, finally a station where they fix it for $17; then the overdrive going on the fritz, Mark saying, "I hope the engine doesn't blow up." Pulling off the highway to fix it. Looked like the Joads headed back, weighted down with cribs and carts and a high chair strapped to the top of the car.

I don't like the crib that we inherited from Paul and Carrie. I think of Lisa whose mother went out and bought her matching furniture, a white modern crib, a bureau and a changing table, brand new rainbow bumpers for her crib. I want things that match, a white modern crib like they have in the window of Nationwide Baby. I don't want to have to sort through the miscellaneous cast-off bumpers I have received, trying to figure out the one I hate least. I swore no lambies and bunnies for my baby, I swore I would not socialize her (and me) into the world of infancy equating inanity, but I forgot that if you take the cast-offs of the world, you have to take what you get.

Trying to convince Mark that no, I really cannot work the foot mechanism to open the crib, it really does require four strong limbs, I know from babysitting, I've never been able to open a crib and yes, I really will hurt my back reaching in there twenty times a day. We really do need to adapt it.

A page or two a day is better than nothing. Still, I wish that I was churning out my novel, the way I was a few weeks ago.

Tomorrow I will make $40 doing a marketing research focus group. I got a check for 46 cents from State. We took $2,000 out of our savings. It is scary to go through it, but it does mean that Mark will be able to take the month after the baby is born off, and my life will not be quite so crazy. Pixie said about being home with a newborn, "You don't just cry every day, you cry all day, every day."

I had to do sixteen hours of community service as a condition of my probation as a result of a sit-in I took part in protesting U.S. actions against Nicaragua. Four four-hour shifts—nothing much for me who used to get up at six in the morning and write, go to work at noon and spend five hours typing ninety words a minute, grab a quick dinner then go to a meeting. That was how I knew I was me. I was the one who was always busy, the one whose phone was always ringing; the one who was always on her way out the door. But I came home from those few leisurely hours of volunteering at the Red Cross aching and almost crying with fatigue.

Lily said that in your last two months your mind goes and you can't do anything. My mind is not going to go. My body may be going, going, gone, but my mind is not going to go. I am going to keep writing every day.

The sink is always filled with dirty dishes. I want my body back, I want my life back. For the first time in my life, I feel my disability as a physical reality, not just as a social condition. I would rather be a quadriplegic than be fatigued like this. Well, OK, not a quad, but a paraplegic.

I am sick of being tired. I am sick of being heavy. I am sick of waiting.

Three

10

"You're not really overdue until you go two weeks past your due date," Laura, the midwife, said.

"You're not really overdue until you go two weeks past your due date," I repeated to Linda, who was calling me every day from San Francisco.

"I'm going nuts waiting for this baby," she said.

"You're going nuts?"

"Are you having twins or triplets?" the woman at the county welfare office had asked me a few weeks before.

"They tell me it's just one," I said.

"*One?*" she said.

I was there to straighten out my Medi-Cal. I was sitting in my Amigo, which looks like a cross between a wheelchair and a go-cart, which I used during the second half of my pregnancy. People were forever stopping me on the street and saying, "What is that?" When I said, "a wheelchair," they would invariably smile very broadly, say, "I'm sorry," and move backwards.

I figured it would be a long wait, so I'd brought the book I was currently reading, *Remembrance of Things Past*. I had just been involved in an elaborate description of a party that Swann had attended – or was it a party to which Swann had not been invited?

This woman wanted to know what my disability was, she wanted to know why I hadn't been vaccinated against polio. The vaccine hadn't been invented yet, I said.

"Oh," she said, as if she didn't quite believe me. "Are they worried you'll pass it along to the baby?"

No, I said, that couldn't happen.

Where was I going to have my baby?

"Santa Monica Hospital," I lied. Hospital births don't require an explanation, but home births do.

"Fucking stupid white bitch," a man sitting a few seats away from me muttered. "Parks her stupid self right in front of the goddamn door." I eased my thumb against the lever of my Amigo, moved forward out of the way.

A few minutes later, a Black social worker opened the door and called out: "James Robertson. James Robertson."

The man mimicked, "'James Robertson. James Robertson.' Fucking stupid faggot." I kept reading Proust, who was describing in meticulous detail the distinction between the pain that comes from the constant thought of the beloved and the pain which is revived by some verb used in a letter from her.

Waiting. When I walked at all, I walked like a cowboy, my baby's head in my pelvis. I had to wake up and get on all fours at night in order to turn over in bed. My sleep was heavy. Again and again, I dreamt about the fish in my aquarium, only in the dreams there are hundreds and hundreds of them, swimming in schools behind vast stretches of glass.

I had been so hoping to be early, so that my mother would fly out to California to be with me. But now the college semester had started, and there was no chance that she would take time off.

*

My due date passed. My midwife advised making love, my mother advised bumpy roads.

"You need a New Hampshire country road," she said over the phone. "That's supposed to do the trick."

"It's a bit far to travel. . . . Were you on time with us?"

"I think . . . pretty much. Of course, Ellen was induced."

My oldest sister was underweight, almost had to be put in an incubator.

"That crazy doctor. He had a favorite nurse he liked to work with, so he induced all his patients so they'd be born on her shift."

Mark and I did find a dirt road – no easy task in L.A. – and drove over it; I rode my Amigo through the bumpy back alleys of Venice. Hot food was supposed to be good too, and I ate ribs with hot sauce, pizza with extra red peppers, Indian food.

"What's the hottest thing on your menu?" I asked the man behind the counter at the Indian cafeteria in Westwood.

"We can make anything as hot as you want it," he said.

I ordered spinach and chicken. "Very hot," I told him. "Very, very hot."

That did it. The next day, I was having contractions, twenty minutes apart. By one in the afternoon, I called Mark at work and told him to come home. Then I called my sister in San Francisco. She and Lisa, my ex-roommate and her lover, flew down.

We bought lilies, Peruvian lilies and tiger lilies, because if it was a girl (and it was going to be a girl) we were going to name her Lily Margaret, after two old friends of mine. "Lily Margaret, and we'll call her Maggie."

Then the contractions stopped, sometime after dinner

that night. We drove up and down a mountain, which started them again. They stopped again. In the movies, people are always in labor and it's dramatic, without question. Real labor can begin like this, contractions that feel like real contractions but don't dilate the cervix; or that dilate the cervix a bit, then stop. We did women's rituals in the dark with a single candle burning, the four of us sitting in a circle (Mark wearing my black slip, to make him an honorary woman) and imagining my cervix opening, opening. I stimulated my nipples, which releases the hormone oxytocin, causing the uterus to contract.

After dinner, Lisa read aloud from *Spiritual Midwifery*, a book written by a midwife on a religious commune in Tennessee called The Farm where labor was considered part of a spiritual process and contractions were called "rushes." "'Somehow I just couldn't get behind shoveling shit,'" Lisa read. "'When we rolled through the gate, I found out why. "Go home, Martin, your wife's havin' a baby!"' . . . The birthing was easy and Eileen was born the next morning. We made out a lot, and I kept Bonnie rubbed out. The baby was small and came out without a lot of pushing . . .

"'When she was just a day old, she lost her voice. It was kind of haunting, hearing such a pure voice go out. Laa, laa, laa, she would cry, each *laa* a little scratchier and fainter than the one before—'"

"I think this is about a baby that dies," Jane said.

Lisa scanned down the page. "Oops," she said, then turned to another piece from the Amazing Birthing Tales section.

The women who live on the Farm all described their births in glowing terms. Their contractions were psychedelic rushes and they rode through their labors on waves of pure white energy. Ina Mae Gaskin, the head midwife, occasionally reprimanded women for being "complainy." I must admit that I became quite complainy as the post due date days stretched into a post-due date week, and beyond.

The standard advice given to overdue women is "Keep busy. Don't sit around waiting to go into labor. Think about other things. Go out to eat. Go to the movies."

Ignoring the presence of a nearly ten-pound fetus camped in your body is not easy. I went out to dinner, I went to the movies, but all through dinner and all through the movies I thought, I wonder when I'm going to go into labor, I wonder when I'm going to go into labor. In fact, I spent a great deal of time staring at my belly and thinking, it could happen any second now. My waters could all of a sudden break. Or a no-doubt-about-it contraction could sweep through my body.

I reread Baraba Katz Rothman's *Giving Birth* and then reread it again. I must have gone over the "Some First Signs of Labor" section in *Our Bodies, Ourselves* a hundred times. You may have diarrhoea, feel an extraordinary sense of energy; *"My body felt different the night before, as if I'd become lighter. . . . "* Did I maybe feel a little lighter? It's not exactly diarrhoea, but . . .

"What are you waiting for?" I asked the fetus. "Maggie, if you come out now, I'll buy you a red bicycle. You'll never have to eat the crusts on your bread."

On Saturday, when I was one week overdue, Mark called Lynn, one of the midwives' assistants, to ask her if it was all right to try castor oil, which was recommended in *Spiritual Midwifery*, or were there any herbs I could try, I was going out of my mind. Castor oil was all right, she said, but we should wait until morning. I took one tablespoon the next morning and threw it up without having anything happen.

Lisa flew back on Tuesday: she had to get back to her job at the crystal animal factory, and she had plans for her birthday on Wednesday.

My next midwife's appointment was on Wednesday. I was eleven days past my due date. Vi, one of the midwives, put a sympathetic arm around my shoulder in the waiting room. Jean, the director of the childbirth center, looked at the board on which women's names and due dates were pinned, and said, "People are starting to look at your name and sigh for you."

"Did you try castor oil?" Laura asked.

"Just once. It was pretty gross."

She told me that I would have to go to the hospital on Saturday – the day when I would be two weeks past my due date – for a non-stress test. A woman I know, Robin, who was also past her due date, has been having them. (She and I had been commiserating with each other lately over the phone.)

For the non-stress test, I would be hooked up to a fetal monitor. Using ultrasound, the machine measures the fetal heart rate and see how it responds to the normal, ongoing contractions of pregnancy. This test is done when women are overdue because the placenta can age and cease to function efficiently, compromising the fetus.

I didn't want my baby exposed to ultrasound, the long-term risks of which are unknown. My oldest sister was a "DES daughter" – that is, they'd given my mother a hormone during her pregnancy, to prevent miscarriage. It turned out that the drug was completely ineffective in preventing miscarriage – and it sometimes caused cancer in the daughters of women who took it. My sister had had cervical cancer when she was in her mid-twenties. I was afraid that in twenty or thirty years they might discover that ultrasound had undreamed of negative consequences.

"Usually scheduling the non-stress test is enough to

make women go into labor," Laura assured me.

She gave me a list of ways of bringing on labor that was given to her by the midwife who had attended the birth of her own daughter Julia, a few months before. "She's a lay midwife who's been practicing for ten years," Laura said.

1 T castor oil in a.m.; next day 2 T in a.m.
tea of pennyroyal, blue cohash — ½ tsp each per cup
breast stimulation
enemas
walking
hands and knees position

"Do whatever you can," I said, as I lay down for the vaginal exam.

"This might hurt," she said.

"I don't care."

She moved her finger around inside of my slightly dilated cervix. She held up two gloved fingers, showing me a little bit of my mucous plug.

Mark and I went right from her office to New Life on Main Street, and were directed to an alcove on the second floor, lined with shelves. The shelves held herbs in one gallon glass jars with white twist-off lids, lined up in alphabetical order. I took the jar of pennyroyal down off the shelf and filled a plastic bag with the crumbled leaves.

A man came in and said, "I'm looking for pennyroyal."

"I've got it right here," I said.

"That helps get rid of fleas?"

That's why I'd heard of it before.

"Give me an ounce," he said.

"I don't work here."

"Oh," he said. "Oh." He picked up the list that Laura gave me.

"That's ways to induce labor."

"Oh," he said. "Oh," and set it down right away.

*

As soon as I got home, I brewed my tea of pennyroyal and blue cohash, and sat sipping it while I talked with Beth, one of the midvives' assistants, about her experiences with midwives in Nicaragua.

"I'm feeling something," I told Beth, "but then I've felt something plenty of times before."

Linda called. "I'm having contractions," I told her.

"This is it. You're going to have this baby tomorrow evening."

"Not tonight?"

"No," Linda said, laughing, "tomorrow night."

My contractions kept on while Jane, my friend Austin and I walked along the Venice boardwalk and stopped at an outdoor cafe near the beach, kept up through our late afternoon snack, and on through dinner.

Mark, Jane, and I watched a three hour show on PBS about abortion that evening. My contractions were fifteen minutes apart and so light that I just set down the stuffed toy I was sewing and said, "Contraction," loudly enough so that Mark would hear me and look at his watch, but not so loudly that I distracted either of them from the TV.

8:28, Mark wrote in his notebook.

"That's it."

45 secs., he wrote.

Since we had been reading *Spiritual Midwifery*, I'd say "rush" instead of contraction every now and again.

On TV a counselor was holding a woman's hand and murmuring, "You're doing really well. It's almost over. You're doing really well."

"Mark," I said, and he looks at his digital watch and adds "10:18" to the column of figures.

"That's it... I wish I hadn't eaten that dinner."

I had put on the white cotton nightshirt with lace trim that had been waiting, carefully ironed, in the closet for weeks. My cheeks were flushed. It's called "mallor," a sign of labor.

Barb called, leaving a message on the tape. Robin's last

non-stress test had shown problems with the fetal heart rate, the doctor had started the labor with pitocin, and she'd ended up having a C-section, a daughter.

The show ended. It was eleven o'clock. It seemed as if my contractions were fading, and Jane started to make me another cup of blue cohash and pennyroyal tea. But then the strongest contraction I'd felt yet coursed through me. I called into the kitchen, "Forget the tea!"

11

We phone the midwives to let them know what's happening, but say that I'm fine, I don't need anyone to come over yet. Jane pulls the futon out from under the couch and goes to sleep on the living room floor. Mark and I nap for about an hour.

Then my contractions are bad enough that I can't sleep. We add numbers to the running tally of the times of my contractions. I spend a lot of time in the bathtub, finding that warm water in labor is not the panacea it has been cracked up to be. Mark reads me a page or so from Proust, because that seems like the kind of thing you are supposed to do when having a home birth. Plus it would make a really good story: "You know, I was so involved in *Remembrance of Things Past* that I gave birth right there in the bathtub."

At four in the morning, the contractions still aren't worse than bad menstrual cramps. Unlike period pains there is a pattern: every five minutes, a minute or so of pulling. And unlike menstrual cramps, there is no murmuring of apologies to an awakened lover, no wondering if I should risk waking roommates with a soothing bath. Labor is the one time in my life when I have not given a thought to anyone else's needs or feelings.

I had learned the Bradley method, not Lamaze. Bradley is the method favored by home birthers. It is less structured than Lamaze, which has its roots in Pavlovian psychology. Rather than learning complex patterns of panting and puffing, Bradley consists of breathing deeply and staying relaxed. (As one of the women in my childbirth class said, "That *can't* be all.")

I'd had a few doubts of my own about Bradley earlier in the day on my walk with Austin and Jane. Austin's daughter Clara had been born two years before, and as we went down the boardwalk she described the elaborate Lamaze breathing that she had used to get her through transition. (Transition is the stage of labor where the woman's cervix dilates the last few centimeters. It is usually said to be the hardest part of labor.)

"What does Bradley say about transition?" Austin asked.

"Oh," I said, "just breathe deeply, stay relaxed. Intensive coaching." It sounded pretty paltry.

But so far, the technique of Bradley seemed to be fine. Bradley, like Lamaze, is named after the male doctor who developed it. The Bradley method is officially known as "husband-coached childbirth." Luanna, our childbirth teacher, was always careful to say "partner" or "coach" instead of "husband" – but that didn't do much to change the underlying concept. The handouts we got in class almost always referred to the laboring woman as "the wife." For instance, "When your wife feels her uterine contraction beginning she should calmly open her chest and inhale as fully as possible three times. . . . " That simple change of nouns moved a woman from an active, independent being to a woman whose status was dependent on that of a man. "Remind your wife to squat every time she goes down to pick up something . . . "

Gee, Dr. Bradley, I don't have a wife.

And that word "coach." It was as if labor were being turned into a sporting event. I conjured up scenes from old movies: Knut Rockne walking among dejected football players in the locker room during halftime, giving them a pep talk that was so moving that they charged onto the field and overcame all the odds to win the big game. Perhaps Jane should get some pom-poms so she could leap around chanting, "Push it out; push it out; all the way out."

On the back of the Bradley workbook, there is the Bradley logo: a heart with a flower growing from it. In the center of the flower is the phrase "Daddy Helped Born Me." Where was Mommy at the time? Out at K-Mart, buying disposable diapers?

But feminist politics aside, Mark and I had practiced our Bradley method, lying in bed at night before we fell asleep, me sitting between his open legs while he squeezed my arm or my shoulder, gradually increasing the pressure, as he said, "Take a deep breath. Now let it out slowly, slowly, slowly. You feel very relaxed. Take another deep breath... "

All through the night, I don't really want or need coaching. The early contractions came in the neat peaks and valleys illustrated in the graphs in the childbirth books. They are like waves, and I imagine that they will get bigger, but still be waves, proceeding into shore in a more or less regular rhythm, cresting, breaking and ebbing.

I've heard that women who were post-polio often had quick labors, so at five in the morning, when I feel chilled and my teeth begin to chatter, I think I may be in transition.

My childbirth educator had joked that most people talked about first and second stage, centimeters of dilation, but she thought the best way of judging how far along a woman was in labor was by the degree of modesty she retained. No one gets to second stage with clothes on. I'd been naked for hours. Mark calls the center, and Merle, one of the midwives' assistants, comes over.

I am sitting up in the rocking chair, with our big pink

quilt wrapped around me, my teeth chattering. Merle checks my blood pressure, which is high, and tells me to lie on my left side, which brings it down immediately. She must think I am in transition, too, because she starts to unpack the birth kit. On the top of Mark's dresser, she sets out one plastic bottle containing olive oil and another one with alcohol, gauze pads and a thermometer, blue and white plastic sheeting. She tells Jane to boil water, and she sets out our bread pan in which to sterilize instruments and our big pottery bowl for the placenta.

Then she does a vaginal exam.

"You're only a finger and a half dilated."

A finger and a half. Nowhere near transition. And I had been one centimeter dilated the morning before, when Laura had checked me. There I had been, feeling like the queen of labor, like one of those legendary women who squats down in the field to give birth.

Merle calls Laura, and I hear her say, "Three centimeters."

"Oh. I thought a finger and a half meant a centimeter and a half." I don't feel *so* bad.

"Do you want me to stay?" Merle asks.

"I think I'll be all right. When do I need to call you?"

"There's no set time – call if your waters break, or if you feel the urge to push. Or any time you feel like you want someone with you."

What happens between the time Merle leaves and when she returns? It's like a memory of pushing a boulder uphill, past a landscape that never varies, on and on and on without change – there is almost nothing to remember. I labor, I labor, I labor, I labor.

Suddenly, instead of waves, labor feels like a hurricane sweeping through my body: wild winds, wild surf, willy-nilly. I am crouched on the floor between the bedroom and the bathroom, swirling, lost.

"Help me," I scream to Mark. "Help me! Help me!"

"I don't know what to do."

Knut Rockne never said that.

"Help me," I moan. "For God's sake, just help me."

Looking back, I realize that there must have been some break between contractions, because there was time to catch my breath and protest, "This isn't the way it's supposed to be. I'm supposed to get a rest. It's not fair, it's not fair, it's not fair," before the next contraction swept through me. But at the time, it seemed that there was no break, no space, no pause.

"Oh, God. Something's wrong. They're coming too fast. It's not supposed to be like this."

"Do you want me to call Merle?"

"Call her – oh, no. No. No. I can't do this. Help me."

There is no bearing, no mooring, no place to hang on to. Only when the contraction eases up can I say, "I'm losing it, I can't. . ." but then the "I" disappears into the relentless, animal physicality of labor.

"Oh, no. No. No. No. No. No."

Merle is there, crouching on the floor next to me, saying, "Yes. Yes. Yes. Yes. Yes. Let it come. Let it open. Yes."

"No," I say. "No."

"Let it open," she says. "Yes. Open."

"No, stop it. Stop it. Stop." Each time she says the word 'open,' I can feel an extra tug in my uterus, as if it were magically responding to her words.

"Yes. Let it open. Open."

"Stop it! My God! Shut up!"

"All right," Merle says. "It's all right."

"It's not all right. It's not all right. They're coming too fast."

"This is a normal labor," she tells me.

"No, it isn't." It doesn't look anything like the homebirth video we saw in childbirth class, a woman humming her way through second stage, saying, "I have to have a bowel movement," and Vi answering, "You go right ahead, dear, that's your baby."

Mark takes over coaching. "Let it come," he says as each contraction hits, and that helps. I am still overwhelmed, but I am no longer losing it. It does not seem possible that this churning is coming from within me.

The only experience I've had that comes anywhere close to labor was a weekend that I spent rafting down the Tuolomne, a wild river in Northern California. When the current grabbed our raft, there was no time to think. Fear and exultation were one. Now, pain and pleasure are melding in a place that is beyond either of them; consciousness is overwhelmed by a wash of raw sensation.

About two hours later, Merle is having trouble hearing the fetal heartbeat with the regular stethoscope, and she leaves for the birth center to get the Doptone, which uses ultrasound to hear the heartbeat.

I feel a gush of fluid during one contraction. "I think my waters just broke."

My sister says yes, they have.

"Is it clear?"

"No. It's sort of brown."

"You have a little bit of meconium staining," Merle says when she gets back. "The baby passed some stool into the amniotic fluid. When its head comes out, we'll tell you not to push, so that we can clean out any meconium that's in its mouth—"

"How do I not push?"

"You just don't push. You'll be able to do it."

"I'm so tired. I just want to sleep and sleep and sleep."

"It'll be a long time before you get to do that," Merle says.

Ah, the baby. I had almost forgotten that when I get done with labor there will be a baby for me to care for. The nights of broken sleep stretch ahead of me, weeks and months of exhaustion, sleepless nights. I have never felt so tired.

I sit on the bed and on the rocking chair; I crouch on all fours; Jane and Mark move the disposable pads so that they stay under me to catch the dripping amniotic fluid and the last of my mucous plug.

"You're doing so well," Merle says.

I feel momentarily proud. Then I remember that is one of the things you're supposed to say to a woman in labor.

"You say that to everybody, don't you?"

"You are doing really well," Merle says.

"But you say that to everybody, don't you?"

"Well, yes," she admits.

"Laura's at another birth," she tells me a while later. "There's a midwife in the South Bay who we put on standby, in case Laura can't make it."

I want Laura. I don't want some stranger. I want Laura.

In the early afternoon, the contractions ease up enough so that Mark and I lie on the bed and nap between them. I wake him at the start of each one,

"Mark."

"Take a deep breath. Let it out slowly. Let it come. Let it come..."

... and we drift back into sleep again.

"Mark."

"Take a deep breath.... You're doing fine... Let it come."

And sleep again.

And then they are rocking me out of sleep, but they are not they, they are me, and I open my eyes between and see the dark wooded room and the white paper shades and the—

"Mark!"

And then there is too much wildness for sleep.

"Let it come."

"Let it come."

"Let it come."

"Can you please say something else? I'm getting sick of that."

And on and on and on and on. Contraction after contraction after contraction. The thought forms in my mind, "I thought it was going to be French, but it's German." I am not at all certain what that means; when this is over, I'll figure it out. And then I sink back into the blankness of labor.

"I want to push."

Merle checks me. "You're only five centimeters."

"Only five?"

"It should go pretty quickly from here."

An hour later, Merle says "I just talked to Laura. The other woman's about to give birth. She should be here soon."

"Your blood pressure's high again. Can you lie down on your left side?"

"I really want to push. . . . "

"You're still not dilated. . . . Try panting to stop yourself from pushing. It'll show you how not to push when the head is born."

"The other woman's had her baby. Laura's repairing a few tears, and as soon as she's done with that, she'll be over."

"Anne, don't push," Merle says.

"I wish Laura would hurry up and get here."

"You know, you won't be able to push when she gets here."

"I know. I just wish she would get here."

Laura arrives. She sits down in the rocking chair, spreading her full skirt around her, the kind of full skirt my mother used to wear when we were kids.

I am talking about drugs: I wish I had some, or maybe just a drink. Can I have a drink? We'd gone out and gotten some liquor, so we'd have some on hand in case we needed it during labor. Mark bought a half-pint of whiskey at the grocery store, and I said, no, I'd never be able to get whiskey down, so he'd bought a half pint of vodka and some coffee liqueur to mix it with.

No, not a drink, it would slow things down.

"I guess the whole neighborhood must know I'm having this baby."

"I don't think so. You've been very quiet."

Laura checks me: two gloved fingers in my vagina.

"You're fully dilated except for an anterior lip. I'm just going to push it back, if that's all right."

"Go ahead."

"You can push with your next contraction."

I am amazed and proud. I have made it through first stage, made it through the painful part of labor, without a drug or without really wanting a drug – at least not all that much.

The next contraction comes. I start to push my baby into the world.

"I thought second stage didn't hurt."

"It depends. I had a harder time with second stage," Laura says.

"This is hard. I thought it wasn't going to hurt."

Once again, the instruments are spread out on Mark's bureau, the water is put on to boil.

"I'm hot," I say. "I'm really hot."

Jane sets up the fan. "We'll have to turn it off when you get closer to having the baby. So it won't get chilled."

Laura sitting in the rocking chair, saying, "You're going to have this baby. You're going to have a beautiful home birth, just the way you want it."

"Anne, when you push, try bending your head down and holding your breath."

I push and push and push. I grunt and moan. And I know, as surely as if I were looking at him, that it is a son I am pushing into the world.

The woman who lives in the house behind us is having a fight—a real fight, not an argument. I come out of contractions to hear high-pitched screaming and once glass shattering.

Earlier, when I'd told her I was having a home birth, she'd said, "Let me know if there's anything I can do." Now I remember that and I want someone to go out back and ask her to be quiet, please, I'm trying to have a baby.

No one seems to want to go.

Jane is looking out the window: "The police are back there," she says. "And the paramedics." I am scared that they are going to hear me groaning and come and knock on the door, try to take me to the hospital.

I kneel on all fours; I squat.

"Anne, when you push, make a real effort to hold the baby where it is between contractions. The head is tilted back, it's making it a little bit harder."

I push, I hold him, I don't let him go back.

"That's good."

"Your blood pressure's gone up again. Can you lie down on your left side?" Mark at my head, Jane lifting up my leg for me as I push.

An hour passes.

"See the top of its head," Laura says to Jane.

"Yes."

"Do you have a mirror?" Laura asks.

I indicate the full length mirror leaning against the wall.

"That'll be good at the end. It's a little big for now."

Someone gets out a small circular mirror, to hold between my legs, but I keep closing my eyes during contractions.

"I have to take a shit."

"That's your baby."

"No. I know its my baby, but I have to shit, too."

"Do you want to try sitting on the toilet? Sometimes that's a good position for second stage."

I sit on the toilet. I push.

I crouch on all fours. After each push, my asshole feels damp and cruddy.

"Can you wipe my butt?" I ask Jane.

I squat. I crouch on all fours and push. I lie on my side. Laura crouches down on the floor next to me to check the fetal heartbeat.

Another hour passes.

"You're going to have this baby... " Laura says.

"Am I going to have it at home?"

"Are you getting tired?"

"Yes," I admit. "Can I have a cup of coffee?"

"I don't think so. I'd be nervous about your blood pressure going up."

"So what if it goes up?"

"You could develop toxemia. Go into convulsions. . . . Maybe Jane could make you a cup of tea. . . . Do you have honey?"

"Yes."

"Put lots of honey in it."

Jane holds the too-sweet tea while I sip it through the straw that came in the birth pack.

Laura goes into the front room to nurse her three-month-old daughter while her husband goes out for sandwiches.

I push. And push. Finally, I start to feel more than just the sensation of having to shit: for one contraction, I have the welcome feeling that I am being split in half.

"Can you wipe my butt?" I say to Jane.

"How are you doing?"

"I need more encouragement, more positive reinforcement."

I am discouraged, and tired. It is starting to get dark out. I sense that everyone else is tired too. Finally, we decide that I will push for another half hour and then think about going to the hospital.

I push for the next half hour, but make little progress. Laura calls Dr. Garnett.

"I'm waiting for Dr. Garnett to call back. I'm going to nurse Julia again."

I pant through some contractions. Merle says, "Keep pushing. Dr. Garnett may try to use the vacuum extractor."

"That was Dr. Garnett. He's going to meet us at the hospital in forty-five minutes."

Jane gets together baby clothes. I put on a nursing bra, my grey dress, my down-at-the-heels running shoes with the Velcro straps that will scarcely fasten across my swollen feet. Laura checks the heartbeat one last time.

Laura's husband wants to use the bathroom, which is

directly off our bedroom. The door between it and our bedroom is shut. After being in labor, literally and psychically naked for hours, it seems modest to the point of eccentricity for him to want the door shut.

"I don't feel bad about going to the hospital. I feel like I gave it my all."

"I think you gave it more than your all," Jane says.

Laura says, "Be prepared for things at the hospital to take a long time. Lots of times women think that things are really going to start moving once they get to the hospital, but they can really drag... "

The transfer to the hospital isn't leisurely, but it certainly isn't rushed either. As I walk to the front door, I stop and flip through the day's mail. Our Springsteen tickets have come, ordered back when we thought we would have a three-week-old at the time of the concert.

At the entrance to Santa Monica Hospital there is a sign: "NO ROLLERSKATES OR BARE FEET ALLOWED IN THE HOSPITAL."

It seems funny that the orderly who pushes the wheelchair out to meet me is in a rush, jabbing at the elevator button with his finger and intoning urgently under his breath, "Come on, come on, come on."

I don't have the strength to explain to him that I have come into the hospital for "failure to progress" and unfortunately, there is no rush, no rush at all.

"How tall are you?" the nurse asks me as soon as I get to the labor room.

"Why?"

"How tall are you?" Her tone of voice indicates that what she is really saying is: You are too small to give birth to this big baby.

"What difference does it make?" I ask.

She turns to Laura and asks, "Did she check in at admissions?"

"No."

"You need to do that."

Mark goes down to the admissions office.

Off with the dress, on with the white hospital gown. Lie down on your back. Lift up the gown. A fetal monitor is strapped around me. A sheet is pulled up over me. The monitor beeps, flashing green numbers. 220, 110, 40.

A nurse palpitates me and says, "She's got a full bladder."

They want to catheterize me, but I insist on trying to pee, although the nurses assure me that I won't be able to. They're right: I am lifted onto a bedpan but I can't go.

"Is there some water you can run?"

Laura finds the bathroom and turns on the water.

"You can't have anything to drink," the nurse says.

"I know. I just thought the sound might help me." You're the one that's so fucking worried about my full bladder – it's not bothering me.

The machine is flashing its numbers. Laura comes and stands between me and the fetal monitor. "These things are awful."

All of a sudden, my legs are being opened and an internal monitor is being inserted into the baby's head.

Laura turns to Jane and says, "Run and get Mark."

I am telling them that it is all right, since my waters have broken, I would rather have an internal monitor than an external one, and avoid exposure to ultrasound. No one pays any attention to me.

"We're still not getting it."

"There's a caput."

A doctor with blonde hair curled softly against her cheeks is bending over me. An oxygen mask is being strapped over my face. I must be fighting it, because Laura is saying, "Anne, it's all right. It's for the baby, it's for the baby."

I am being catheterized and shaved. I remember that two nurses were shaving me at once, one scraping off the

right side of my pubic hair, the other scraping off the left –
can that be right? Behind her glasses, Laura's eyes are thick
with tears.

Again and again I go over that first quarter of an hour
at the hospital. But it's all disjointed, in bits and snatches
that don't fit together. Asking Jane and Mark, do you remember what happened? After I said that, what did she
say?

I still can't remember that Mark came back from the
admissions office, that the people I love were with me. I
see Laura and Jane leaning against the window ledge, dis-
tant, even though I have been told that they were with me,
holding my hand.

For a long time, I could remember turning to Laura
and asking her about the C-section, saying, "Is this all
right?" and her saying yes, but I couldn't remember being
told that I should have a C-section. And then it came back
to me: Dr. Resnick, a short man in green scrubs, with a fat
gold chain around his neck, introducing himself and putting two fingers on my carotid artery, saying, "We're not
getting a fetal heartbeat. I'm not sure what we were picking up earlier, whether it was the baby's heartbeat or
yours. We were picking up a heart rate of 110 – your heart
rate's 110.

"Your baby's in severe distress. You can wait until Dr.
Garnett gets here, and he'll do a crash C-section or I can
do it now."

I turn to Laura and say, "Is that all right?"

She nods her head and says, "Yes."

"I have scoliosis." I still do not realize that this is not
like the C-sections they described in childbirth education
class, I still think that Mark will hold my hand and they
will hand me the baby to nurse after he is born. I think

they will try an epidural, which will leave me awake – but which can be complicated by scoliosis.

"We don't have time to try an epidural. We have to give you general."

They are running, pushing the labor bed with me on it, down the hallway as he speaks to me.

Outside the door of the operating room, the anesthesiologist tells me, "There are risks to this procedure, but I don't have time to tell you what they are."

"It's all right. I know what they are."

"Get some Betadine on her belly," the doctor with the gold chain around his neck is shouting.

I shout down the corridor, "Mark, I love you."

Another mask over my face. I am afraid they are going to start giving me anesthesia through the mask, instead of putting me out first with an injection in my hand. But then I feel a needle going into my hand...

12

Green oxygen mask still over my face.

Beep. Beep. Beep. Electronic.

Mark's watch? He has one of those electronic ones; one little gizmo broke and now it beeps every morning at eight, there's no way to stop it.

No, this is not sleep. Not his watch beeping. Something else.

Surfacing.

Laura, Jane, and Mark standing next to my bed. Another room, not the OR. Green oxygen mask over my face.

And down again.

And up.

"You had a boy."

"Is he all right?"

"Yes," Mark says.

"He's in intensive care," Laura says.

I reel back into the thick chemical sleep.

Beep. Beep. Beep. Beep.

Machine above my head. Beeping out my pulse or my respiration.

"Can I take this off?" I can hear my words, muffled behind the oxygen mask and slurred from anesthesia. I am not as out of it as I sound, I want to say, but in some cloudy corner of my mind I realize I will sound like a drunk proclaiming sobriety in a sodden voice.

A nurse comes in, takes the mask off.

"Can you turn that beeping down?"

She turns the machine off. "There."

"Is he OK?" I ask Laura.

"They're working on him."

"What happened?"

"He has meconium aspiration," Laura says. "Do you know–"

"It happened to my friend's baby." Meconium is a fancy word meaning shit. Fetal shit. Aspiration is a fancy word meaning breathing. He breathed shit into his lungs.

Yes, I say, my friend's baby is fine now. Almost a year old. I saw him when I was in New York, in April.

Jane and Laura tell me that the doctor has given Laura a really hard time. He came out of the OR shouting at her, demanding to know if she were licensed, why we hadn't come to the hospital sooner.

Coming from the other side of the curtain, I can hear the groggy voice of a woman and the struggling cry of a newborn baby.

"Look at her. Look at her," the father and grandparents repeat. "Look at those eyes. Look at her."

Jane leaves to call my mother to ask her to come out to California.

From the other side of the curtain: "Look at those eyes. . . . Oh, sweetie. Don't cry. Don't cry."

"I'm Dr. Holtzmann." The accent is not exactly German – maybe Swiss or Belgian. Another short doctor. He is saying, "Your baby is very, very sick. He had very severe meconium aspiration. It happens when a baby is in distress. The anal spincter relaxes . . . the baby passes the meconium in its colon. If it's not getting enough air through the placenta, it will try to take a breath while still in the womb and breath in the meconium. It causes a very severe chemical pneumonia.

"We put him on a ventilator as soon as he was born,

but he was fighting the ventilator, so we had to give him Pavulon. It's a drug like curare – it paralyzes him completely. We know from what adults tell us that it can be unpleasant, so we're giving him some narcotics to sedate him, too."

"Look at those little hands," the woman on the other side of the curtain repeats in amazement.

"Your baby was very severely asphyxiated. So he's going to have some brain damage. We don't know how severe that's going to be."

He is telling me that my baby may die, but he does not say that. "Your baby may not live," he says. As if not living were somehow not as bad as dying.

From behind the fog of drugs and pain and exhaustion, from behind the numbness spreading over me, I struggle to say, "I know it's hard to give a number, but can you give us some idea of what his chances are?"

"I really can't do that."

One in a hundred of living? One in a hundred of dying?

"Brain damage," I say. "So we're talking about the possibilty of c.p., epilepsy – "

"Yes. Or retardation. . . . Did you take any drugs when you were pregnant?"

"No. My sister's a DES daughter, I was religious about not taking drugs." I didn't even chew sugarless gum, I was worried about the chemicals. Didn't pump my own gas, or use cleaning products for the first four months.

"He looks okay, he has all his toes and fingers," Dr. Holtzmann says.

Webbed toes, an extra thumb, I wouldn't care.

"He may develop a condition called persistent fetal circulation, where the blood is still circulating as it was when he was in the womb." Only he says, "as it vas vhen he vas in the vomb. Vhen it goes to the lungs, it doesn't pick up much air." He reminds me of the insipid Nazis on Hogan's Heroes.

"You'll be able to see him in a little while. We're still working on him. Do you have any other questions?"

I need to seem competent, on top of things. I think that if I can just stay on their good side, if I can just appear rational, then things will be easier. (I must have succeeded, because later, in the nursing notes, I read, "Mother awake and asking appropriate questions.")

"We love him very much," I say. "Do everything you can for him."

Dr. Holtzmann leaves. Jane is there. "Ma said she might come out."

"Call her back. Tell her she has to be on the next plane." My baby might not live. My baby might not live. My baby might not live.

She comes back in a few minutes. "The line was busy," she says. I look at the clock on the opposite wall. It's ten-thirty here; one-thirty on the East Coast. Who is she talking to?

Laura and Jane standing on my left side; Mark is sitting on my right.

"Is this the worst thing that's ever happened to you –" I ask, then think maybe that question is too personal and add, "professionally?"

"Oh, Anne," she says. "I've never had a problem with a mother or a baby before."

"How many births have you done –"

"I've been at hundreds. And I've had sole responsibility for more than fifty."

"When this is over," I tell her, "we'll talk and talk and talk." I want to hold on to her hand, a mooring of gentleness and care in this sea of beeping machines and this doctor who says, "Your baby might not live," with the same tone of voice he would use to tell me, "Your baby has a skin rash." Later there will be time for the luxury of doubt, and questioning and anger. Now I only know I need her to get through this.

Mark is sitting alone in the chair off to the side, crying.

"Both of Mark's parents died when he was a kid. He was always afraid if we had a baby that it would die."

"I didn't know that," Laura says.

When you read those tearjerker stories in the women's magazines, people always say, "I heard about terrible things happening to other people, but I never thought it would happen to me." Me, I felt just the opposite: all kinds of terrible things had happened to me and Mark. I thought that gave us some sort of protection. I thought we'd paid our dues. From here on out life would pull no more dirty tricks. There would be no more sucker punches.

I used to hold him in the night and say, "Don't worry. Everything bad has already happened to us." Me, I said that. Me, who thinks that if there were a God he would play dice with the universe.

Laura is making phone calls from the phone in the recovery room: calling her husband, calling the medical director of the birth center, calling Harvey Karp, our pediatrician. Harvey will be here to see us at seven tomorrow morning.

Jane calls my mother again. The phone had been busy because she was calling the airlines. Her plane gets in at eleven tomorrow morning.

"Look at those little fingers! Can you believe those little fingers!" the other new mother is saying.

"This is hard," I say.

Jane goes out to the nurses' station, to see if one or the other of us can be moved from the recovery room, so I will not have to hear her joyful voice say again, "Look at those eyes!"

"I got yelled at," she says when she comes back. Later on, she tells me that the nurse on duty snapped, "That woman has a right to her baby." "I wasn't asking you to take her baby away," Jane says, but the nurse had turned back to the papers on her desk.

"Hi. I'm Kate." A nurse in blue scrubs. "We're going

to get you cleaned up so you can go down to the ICU."

"I don't care about being clean, I just want to see my baby."

"We need to preserve some decorum. Anyhow I'm not sure they're ready for us yet in the ICU."

I lie there while she sponges off the blood and sweat and Betadine, while she puts a sanitary napkin between my legs, "Can you lift up your hips?" I haven't worn a sanitary belt since junior high school.

"Your son is a real fighter," she is telling me. "He almost died in the OR. . . . " She says that Mark can spend the night, sitting in a rocking chair next to the baby's incubator. "The baby will hold on to your finger," she tells Mark.

She is sponging off my face, she is tying the straps of the johnny.

Oh, please, just hurry, hurry, hurry.

All five of us – the nurse, Laura, Mark, Jane and I, go into the neonatal ICU. I am still on the gurney, with an IV pole attached to it and an IV dripping into my hand.

I remember that, and the blue and white card with an illustration of a teddy bear and blocks on it taped to one of the monitors. It said, "Boy Finger."

I remember that Mark said, "His name is Max." His voice was urgent, almost angry.

And I remember that when Mark said that I felt a sharp thrust of sadness and finality pierce my fog of numbness. This really is our baby.

What I don't remember is Max himself.

But Mark did take a photograph of him.

Sometimes I look at those early photographs of Max and imagine the people who worked at the camera store where they were developed seeing them. "Oh, my God," I hear them saying. "What is that? Why would anyone want to take a picture like that?"

Here is a photograph of Max that first night. His blond hair and his skin and nails are stained with meconium; green-black clumps of it are in his hair. His face too is stained, but I think, looking at the picture, that it must be with Betadine. A respirator is taped across his mouth. There is an IV in his left hand. Four electrodes are glued to his chest. The one that measures his heart rate is shaped like a Valentine's Day heart. A tube runs from his belly button, and an IV line runs from his foot. He is catheterized.

He is in a warmer. This is a table-like bed with a radiant heater above. One of the wires on his chest is measuring his body temperature: the radiant heater varies its temperature according to that reading. He lies alone and naked. The warming table allows the medical personnel more access than a traditional incubator.

Paralyzed, Dr. Holtzmann had said, completely paralyzed, and I thought, hey, that's OK, some of my best friends are quadriplegics. I had imagined him like a quad, a motionless body and a fully alive head. But no, Dr. Holtzmann meant complete paralysis: his eyes can't open, even his tear ducts are paralyzed, so that his eyes have to be smeared with artificial tears.

"It's all right to touch him," a nurse says. I try to find a place on his body where there are no tubes and wires, where there is room for my hand.

My sorrow has anesthetized me. I stare numbly at him.

Then I am wheeled into my room. A plaque on the wall says, "The Glenn Ford Pavilion." A nurse asks me if I want a pain killer and I say yes. Yes, I want a pain killer. Is there such a thing? She rolls me gingerly onto my side and eases a needle into my buttock. I fall asleep immediately.

No, my son Max did not slip out from between my legs in our redwood paneled bedroom. He did not look into my eyes as I put him to my breast. Laura, Jane, Mark, the baby and I did not all climb onto the bed for a group picture, arms looped around shoulders on a rumpled bed. We did not all sit down to the French chocolate birth-day cake that I had baked while I was waiting to go into labor.

Waking out of a thick sleep. A nurse in blue scrubs is taking my temperature, my blood pressure, my pulse, giving me another shot of Demerol, and down.

Again. Two fingers against my wrist. Check the IV line. "There," warm hands helping me to turn on my side. Why does the alcohol swab before a shot always feel cool? Quick prick. Back down into the dark.

A nurse is standing next to my bed. Light comes from the hallway. She is telling me that Max is the same. I understand that is good news: he has not stopped living, they have not lost him.

The room is light. Morning. I see that I have a roommate. They have brought my roommate's baby to her. The emptiness of my arms is a physical ache. I want to ask this stranger if I can hold her baby, to tell her: my baby's in intensive care, he might die, can I just hold yours? But I am afraid she will say no. Afraid she will think I am jinxed, I've got cooties, the bad luck is catching.

Will my baby really die here, here in this land of palm trees and rollerskates, here in this wilderness of drive-in taco parlors and flashing electric signs? Here in this place that is not my home? I know that if Max dies here, I will leave, leave and never, ever, ever come back.

Mark comes into my room. Why do I remember these odd details—that he was wearing the green jacket I gave him for Christmas the year before last—while everything else is such a blur? We must have held each other. That comes back to me now, memories of my head against your shoulder, the two of us clinging to each other; how usually your body has a smell that is faint, slightly flat – a gentle smell; and how all that long weekend you smelled so sharp and harsh.

You had been to see Max already. You tell me he is beautiful.

"He's going to live. I know he is," you say.

Me, I don't hope for life – that seems like too much, tempting fate. I just hope that I will get to see Max's eyes open before he dies.

Harvey and Laura arrive. We have only met Harvey once before, interviewing him with a list of questions that we culled from childbirth education class and books for prospective parents. I'd liked the answers to all his questions, but mostly I'd liked him because he looked as if he could have been a friend of mine in high school, a skinny man with a wispy beard who I could have smoked dope with in the backseat of my parents' VW in 1968.

"I just saw Max," he says. "He's holding his own."

He tells me Max has developed persistent fetal circulation, he explains to me again about meconium aspiration. . . .

"Can you give us an idea of what his chances are?"

He pauses for a moment. I can tell he doesn't want to answer that question, but he says, "I would say he has a better than fifty percent chance of pulling through."

I strip the sugar coating from that pill. Fifty-fifty. Well, at least I know.

The next few days will be the critical period, he is saying.

They have no idea at this point what sort of damage he will have, and it will be a long time before we do know. . . . He may have severe problems or he may be one of those kids who thumbs his nose at the medical profession.

"You came in on a very anti-home birth shift... The

122

problem in your labor may have been something that happened on the way to the hospital, or shortly after you got here. It just doesn't seem that likely that Laura would have missed every contraction where the heartbeat was dropping."

"All you can do now is pray," Harvey says.

All you can do now is pray, except I can't, I don't believe in God.

He tells me to take my pain killers: it is important for me to be up and around. He gives me a hug before he leaves; he tells me he will be back later on.

My breakfast tray arrives. Since I am on a liquid diet, I get a carton of milk – which I can't drink because I am lactose intolerant – a plastic container of reconstituted orange juice, a cup of beef broth and a square of red jello on a white plastic plate. I drink the orange juice.

Mark leaves to go see Max.

Dr. Resnick, the doctor who performed the C-section, comes in next. He struts around at the foot of my bed. Laura is perched on the window ledge. What went wrong, I ask him. I wasn't getting good medical care, he says. I should have been given a glucose tolerance test, he says, especially with that big a baby. I may have had diabetes of pregnancy, and typically those babies don't do well when they go past their due date – and I was two weeks overdue.

I need to get up and walk, he says.

Can he order me a walker, a wheelchair, I'm post-polio, usually I walk with a cane.

No, I can't take a shower yet.

When he leaves the room, I turn to Laura and say, "Don't worry. I take what he says with a grain of salt." What I mean is a pound of salt.

"You weren't spilling sugar into your urine," she says. "Well, you know that. And for the birth center, because we don't restrict women's eating, that's not such a big baby."

Dr. Garnett, my back-up doctor whom I have never

met before, arrives. He too has a gold chain around his neck, although a much thinner one than Dr. Resnick. He is telling me that when he got the call from the hospital, saying how bad things were, he made it from his office in Beverly Hills to Santa Monica Hospital in seven minutes.

Mark comes back.

"How is the baby doing?" Dr. Garnett asks.

"OK," Mark says. "The same."

"How much oxygen is he on?"

"A hundred percent."

"A hundred percent oxygen," Dr. Garnett says, and adds in a whisper, "Oh, boy."

I had known everything about childbirth. Suddenly I knew nothing about what was going on. I was so muddleheaded. It wasn't until nearly a week later when my friend Maureen, who's a doctor, came to visit me, that I began to get things a little bit sorted out. "You understand, don't you," she had said, "that there are separate things going on – the meconium aspiration and the possibility of brain damage?" It was so simple and obvious, but I hadn't understood it until that moment. Until that moment, Max's condition had seemed as unspecific as the illnesses in Victorian novels: crises that were as much of the soul as of the body.

When Dr. Garnett muttered that, "Oh, boy," under his breath, I thought that mysterious phrase "one hundred percent oxygen" had to do with the degree of brain damage he had sustained.

"With that kind of damage, you must have been having a problem for a while," Dr. Garnett says. "It was the worst meconium we've ever seen: it was all over everything, the placenta, the baby . . .

"I was talking with Gary Richwald on the phone last night about this." (Gary is the medical director of the childbirth center.) "He was crying . . . I said, 'Gary, what are we going to do? Not do home births anymore? Board up the Alternative Birthing Centers? Because this same thing could have happened in an alternative birth center, right here in the hospital.'

"You know," he says, "if you'd known when you left your house at nine in the morning that the other guy was going to run a stop sign at nine-fifteen and plow into you, you never would have left the house. Obviously, if you'd known this was going to happen, you never would have started out at home. . . .

"He's going to have some damage. You just don't go through trauma like that and come out without problems. You know, maybe he would have had an IQ of 120 and instead he'll have an IQ of 70. Or maybe it would have been 170, and instead it'll be 120." He gives me a hug; he tells me to pray.

If I'd squatted during second stage would this not have happened? Could the herb tea that I'd drunk have caused this? Or maybe if I'd gone into labor sooner – maybe if I'd drunk the tea the week before? Was it that I hadn't pushed hard enough? Or was it that my pelvis was too narrow? If I'd lain down in the backseat of the car rather than sitting up in the front?

Why? It's not any cosmic answers that I want, not any "Why me?" but a concrete practical why.

It seems that things were fine until we got to the hospital. Could it have been lying on my back in the labor room that did it? Maybe if I had never come into the hospital at all? How had we decided to come to the hospital anyhow? I could remember saying, "I don't feel bad about going to the hospital – I feel like I gave it my all." But I couldn't remember any discussion before then of transferring; only that we were suddenly doing it.

Alone with Laura, I ask her, "Was it that my pelvis was too narrow?"

"No," she says, "it wasn't a problem with your pelvis."

"Was it that I didn't push hard enough?"

"Oh, Anne," she says, "it wasn't anything that you did or didn't do."

Was it something that you did or didn't do, Laura? Dr. Garnett said there were a couple of "red flags": my isolated rises in blood pressure, the meconium stained fluid, the fact that I was a fairly small woman giving birth to a large baby, the dip in the fetal heart rate. None of them alone was a reason to bring me into the hospital, but adding them all together, perhaps we should have decided to come in sooner.

I think of those paper sheets that were spread under me: they would show the color of the fluid, how dark the meconium staining was. Laura and Merle gathered them up and deposited them in the wastebasket. I think of asking my sister Jane to dig them out and save them. If I sue, they would be evidence. The image flashes across my mind of them being displayed in court, like a blood-stained bedsheet used to be displayed to the wedding guests.

Four

13

This is the sink outside the neonatal intensive care unit. Mark shows you what to do. In the cupboard above the sink are the yellow gowns. He takes down one for himself and one for you. You put it on so it ties up the back; it looks a little bit like a priest's robe. He pushes up his sleeves; you push up your sleeves.

He takes two packets from the boxes on the shelf above the sink. He hands you one. Tear it open. Here is a plastic scrub brush and a sponge embedded with yellow soap, a plastic pick with which to clean your nails.

No, there is no wheelchair accessible sink outside the NICU. Rise slowly to your feet, wavering. Clean your nails, scrub your hands. Rinse off the yellow-orange foam.

This is the NICU. There is a handwritten sign on the door we go through that says, "DO NOT USE THIS DOOR." It is a large room: eight or ten incubators. Four of them are on this side of the nurses' station, where Max is. I roll past Christopher and Neda, those scrawny premies (think of two pounds of butter, formed into a human shape) with impossibly thin arms and legs. The smallest, eviscerated chicken at the supermarket counter weighs more than they do. They look worse than the worst pictures of starving Biafran or Ethiopian children you have ever seen.

I feel a wave of envy toward their mothers. I wish I had

a premie. They move, their eyes are open, their mothers can hold them.

Here is Max. He is the Goliath of the NICU, at 9 lbs., 3 ozs. His eyes are still closed and smeared with artificial tears. His chest moves up and down with the respirator. The machine above his warming table shows his heartbeat and respiration, blood pressure. His blond hair is still stained with meconium and his long ragged fingernails are still stained, too. They look like a derelict's fingernails.

The nurses have shifted his position. That is the only thing that has changed. That, and the fact that there is one more tube. This one runs from his chest, just below his left nipple. That's right, I remember now, Dr. Holtzmann came in and told me that Max had a pneumothorax, air escaped from his lung into his chest cavity. They have put in a chest tube to drain the air. I am glad that I do not know yet that the popular term for pneumothorax is "lung collapse."

I am blank: that is why I remember all this so well. I can close my eyes and reel it back. An Andy Warhol film where the camera just keeps going, taking it all in. Everything – the breakfast tray with the jiggling red jello, the body of my maybe-dying son – getting the same amount of attention.

Taped to Christopher's incubator is a handlettered square of paper with his name and a four-color rainbow drawn with magic markers. The floor of the intensive care unit is linoleum, speckled pale pinks and blues and greys. It is surprisingly dirty: a few odd clumps of dust, the torn remains of plastic packets that once contained wipes or needles.

See, I remember everything. My writing teachers always said that I was good at those telling details. Isn't it odd how my mind keeps working? Isn't it odd how my heart keeps pumping, even when there's no blood in my veins, just painkillers and shock?

Max. Lying there. His chest moving up and down. But

it is not his chest moving, it is the respirator that is moving his chest. Red marks on his skin where electrodes have been placed. "Those will fade in a day or two," a nurse tells me.

If he lives, I think.

Maybe they will fade even if he dies, one of those physiological processes that seems to continue after death. In Frida Kahlo's biography, I read that a friend of hers knelt and kissed her corpse, and goosebumps appeared on Kahlo's dead flesh. "She's alive," the friend cried. Diego Rivera had to—

An alarm going off. As insistent as the heel of a hand leaning on a horn, a smoke detector's blare. The nurses go through their routines, not seeming to notice or care. One of the lines on the monitor above Christopher's incubator has flattened out to a long blue blip. I have watched enough television to know what this means: it means death.

What the hell is going on here? Why doesn't someone do something? Why doesn't anyone notice?

"Mark," I say.

"Look at the baby," he says, an old pro already.

Christopher, writhing in his incubator, is decidedly not dead. A lead has fallen off.

First I rolled in a wheelchair, and then I walked leaning on a walker and then finally with just my cane past the nurses' station to the neonatal intensive care unit. I would sit there until I was just about to fall asleep from the combination of the warm stale air in that enormous room and the Demerol in my veins; and then I would roll back across the hall to my room.

A new room, no longer the Glenn Ford Pavilion. If Mark sleeps with me there, then no one else can stay in the other two beds. So they have moved me to a smaller room, one that happens, thankfully, to be closer to the NICU. A few feet less of hallway to walk makes a big difference after a C-section.

My new room has the most garish wallpaper imaginable – gigantic orange-yellow blossoms against a pink background, with impossible lime-green leaves. (Is there really an interior decorator, living in Beverly Hills and driving a Mercedes, who has made money from picking out this wallpaper? "I like this," I imagine her saying, "It's so cheerful. Very up.")

I would sleep for a while beneath that gaudy riot of flowers. Wake up to turn over, move carefully; when you have to cough, press a pillow against your incision. Awake, I would move again past the nurses' station and across the hall to the NICU.

The nurses keep calling me Mrs. Finger. The doctors keep telling me to pray.

Mrs. Finger is my mother and I'm an atheist.

Then here she is. The real Mrs. Finger. My mother has appeared out of the fog. She is crying. "I was so glad when Jane met me at the airport to know that – everything was still the same. . . . I just stopped and looked in the window. He's a beautiful baby."

People kept saying that to me all weekend long. "He's such a beautiful baby."

And every time I heard it, a voice in my head answered back, "He'll make a lovely corpse."

My mother is here at last, but then her being here makes no difference. Now there are three women hovering near me in the fog, Jane and Laura and my mother, but they are all blurred.

Mark, you are the only one who is real to me. All weekend long, we say the same words back and forth to each other, like a chant:

I say: "I hope I get to see his eyes before he dies."

And you say: "He's going to live. I know he is."

We sleep at night on two hospital beds pushed together, our hands stretched across the gap. If our hands move in sleep and we are no longer touching, we wake instantly, to touch again.

Hour after hour, we sit next to Max as he lies not seeing, not responding, not moving. "He can feel you, he can hear your voice," the nurses keep telling us. "Look, his heartbeat goes down when you're talking to him." I looked at the blue monitor with the fancy screen above his bed, the series of moving lines. "See," Florrie says, pointing to one of the wavering lines, "that's his heart."

At each meal, another plastic tray, pale yellow or lime green, appears with jello, milk, juice and beef broth. The dietician comes to see me: I tell her I am lactose intolerant, and ask for acidophilus milk, which I can digest. The next morning on my tray instead of a red and white carton of milk I find a blue and yellow carton of Mocha Mix. The label reads: Water, partially hydrogenated soybean oil, corn syrup, mono & diglycerides, soy protein, dipotassium phosphate, polysorbate 60, sodium stearoyl lactylate, salt, artificial color (beta carotene), artificial flavor. It does not contain more than two percent of the recommended daily allowance of protein or of any vitamin or mineral known.

The lactation consultant comes to see me.

"Here you go," she says. She is handing me five or six xeroxed sheets, stapled together.

"I don't know if any one told you, I have a special situation... "

"Yes, I know," she says quickly. "There's a breast pump you can use." And she leaves the room. Before I get a chance to ask her: I don't know if I want to encourage my milk to start because won't it be worse if he dies? What does it feel like if your baby dies and milk comes pouring out of your breasts to feed a corpse? How long would it take for the milk to dry up? Suppose I didn't start pumping now, but waited a few days to see if he was going to live?

That whooshing is the sound of the breast pump. An electric motor, you put a cup over your breast and turn on the machine. A steady rhythm, back and forth. A machine sucks my breast instead of a baby's mouth.

Max needs a blood transfusion, because they have to take so much out for tests. I ask Dr. Holtzmann if we can use my sister's blood, if it's the right type. He is telling me that the blood supply is very safe now. I know, I just feel safer with lesbian blood. I just like the idea of my sister's blood running in his veins.

After a while, I stopped asking questions because even as they were being answered the words would start to get tangled up in my head.

This is a respirator. Yes, that I understand. Barb's brother is on a respirator; Paul uses one at night. Respirator.

Normal room air is twenty-one percent oxygen. You've just learned that. See, there's something valuable about this experience. You've learned a new fact. Maybe someday you'll go on *Jeopardy* and the big question will be, "What percentage of air is made up of oxygen?"

Max is on one hundred percent oxygen. That means that pure oxygen is being fed through his respirator tube to his lungs. (Still, it is not enough.) Respirator. Oxygen. One hundred percent. Got that? Got it.

Curare is a – No, the drug that begins with "P" is a curare-like drug. It causes paralysis; without life support, it would cause death.

Phenobarbitol, you know that word. Isn't there a

134

singer in a San Francisco punk band whose name is Phenobarbitol? Or maybe she writes for *Processed World*? Phenobarbitol is a downer, a sometimes drug of abuse or recreation. Later a friend will volunteer, "Oh, phenobarb, I did that once. When I was in high school I'd do anything–I even did Thorazine. Phenobarb was awful, my body felt too heavy to move. I just sat there for hours." Phenobarbitol.

Max is being given phenobarbitol to prevent seizures, which he may or may not have had, they can't tell because he was paralyzed by the drug that begins with "P" and isn't phenobarbitol. "Ve did an EEG on him," says Colonel Klink, "und it showed some abnormalities, but ve veren't really sure if it vas seizure activity or nut. Dose portable EEGs sumtimes pick up a lot uf electrical activity dat's just in de air."

(Oh, that awful voice in my head. The one that keeps saying, "He'll make a lovely corpse." The one that keeps making fun of his accent. He's not German. Even if he were German, that hardly makes him a Nazi.)

The opposite of the verb intubate is extubate.

Intubate means to put a tube from a respirator down into a person's windpipe. Extubate means to remove such a tube. Extubate, a verb with a regular conjugation. I extubate, you extubate, he/she/it extubates. The past participle of extubate is extubated. See, this is all very logical and orderly, this all makes a lot of sense.

Persistent fetal circulation. You know those words. "Persistent" means of an action or condition: continued, continuous, constant. "Fetal" means: of or pertaining to or of the nature of a fetus. "Circulation" is the circuit of blood from the heart through the arteries and veins, and back to the heart. Continued, continuous, constant, from the heart through the arteries and veins, and back to the heart, in the manner of a fetus, through the arteries and veins and back to the heart again, continued, continuous, constant. Persistent fetal circulation.

How many times has this been explained to you now? Four, five? In the fetal state, blood circulates but does not need to pick up oxygen from the lungs, as oxygen is being supplied through the placenta. In the condition known as persistent fetal circulation, the baby, not having drawn a breath outside the womb, believes it is still in the womb, and its blood continues to circulate without picking up enough oxygen from the lungs.

Can you explain that to me just one more time?

PO_2 levels are... I don't know. I do know that little grey machine is the one that flashes out his PO_2 levels. I just don't know what that means. I just can't remember whether it's good when they go up or good when they go down.

I do know that if he dies, I will think that technology is monstrous, inhuman, a mad scientist's creation; and if he lives, I will think it is miraculous.

During the course of the weekend I see a yellow sheet of paper that says:

Failed home birth
Meconium aspiration + + + +
Severe asphyxia

I have failed home birth. I have not been able to give Mark a healthy child. Yes, I really thought that. Those words were in my head: give him a child. I thought that he might leave us, two cripples, an embarrassment. Here comes that poor man, saddled with a gimp lover and a retard son. I know what those feelings are, they're internalized oppression; there are words for them too.

Max, those first awful days, when we didn't know if you would live or not, when everyone kept saying, "Your baby has been severely asphyxiated and we don't know how bad the damage is going to be," I had moments of not knowing whether I wanted you to live or not.

I still believed in all the things I have always believed in: the rights of disabled infants, the value of disabled lives. Yes, I still believe in those. I just didn't know what I could cope with: twenty seizures a day? Inability to make eye contact? Changing diapers for twelve years?

Harvey did say, "Or maybe he'll be one of those kids who thumbs his nose at the medical profession." And Dr. Garnett said, "Maybe he would have had an IQ of 170, and instead it'll be 120." I let myself forget that the whole concept of IQ is a hereditarian notion derived from the eugenics movement; that it has been used to suppress people of color and disabled people, that I do not believe it is valid as any sort of a measure of human value. Instead, I think about how I always did so well on IQ tests: any kid of mine is destined to have an astronomically high IQ, so even with severe damage he will still be OK.

"Ve vill be able to tell a liddle bit more vhen de baby comes off de Pavulon." But still, everyone keeps telling me, it will be a long wait, years, before we really know much of anything.

If he lives.

And still that ache in my arms. Not pain. Almost its opposite. An absence of needed sensation.

There is Robin's baby. Robin who was overdue with me, who had a C-section like me. She is here at this hospital. She would let me hold her baby.

One of the nurses goes down the hall to ask Robin if she and her daughter will come see me. They're taking a nap now. Then later another message: she will be here in just a bit. No, a little bit longer, she's nursing the baby now. This is hospital time; post C-section time, a journey down five rooms takes all afternoon.

*

137

All of us shuffling slowly, bellies slashed open, they use staples now not stitches, we sit on the toilet while our bowels hiss and coil, and wait for the shit to expel itself. We walk slowly hands pressed just against our pubic bones, as if we are trying to keep ourselves from spilling out. We have bikini cuts, the doctors tell us. A low scar that will be invisible behind our pubic hair. Yes, we can still wear a bikini. The doctors think this will make us happy.

I didn't want one more scar, and it doesn't make any difference whether it's fat or thin, pale or purple, hidden by my pubic hair or not.

I wanted to give birth, not have my child cut out of me.

Finally Robin and Gavrielle arrive. I hold Gavrielle. It feels as if a missing part of my body has been restored.

Robin is saying she is glad she has a girl, if it had been a boy the bris – the circumcision ceremony – would have to have been held on Yom Kippur, when they were fasting, and what's a party without food?

This is ordinary conversation. It comforts me. Mark takes a picture of me holding Gavrielle. A white bundle, she could be my baby.

Harvey calls. I balance Gavrielle in one arm, tuck the phone receiver under my chin. He tells me that some number is holding steady.

"Is that a good sign?" I ask.

"It's a neutral sign," he says.

There are faces appearing out of the fog, Jane and my mother and Laura, and voices crackling over telephone wires or coming out of people's mouths. Laura tells me that Vi is a devout Catholic and has organized a prayer circle to pray for Max. Mark's sister, Ruth, calls and reads to him from the Bible.

If I believed in God I could make deals with him. I read

in the newspaper when I was a kid about a woman whose husband had been taken prisoner in the Bay of Pigs invasion, and she promised God she would shave her head if he were released. There was a picture of her, bald-headed and grinning in the *Providence Evening Bulletin*. If I believed in God I could say, "Listen, if you let him live I'll stop eating meat, I'll give up coffee, I'll never complain about hearing him cry, I won't honk my horn and swear at other drivers, I promise I won't, I won't make bitchy remarks anymore, not even in my head, I promise, I'll be nice to everyone all the time, I'll walk on my knees from Fairbanks, Alaska, to Tierra del Fuego, I'll eat old bubble gum that I find on the sidewalk, all right, I'll eat dog shit off the sidewalk, I'll put an ad in the classifieds thanking Saint Jude, if you just let him live . . . "

Something is happening to my baby. He's a balloon baby, so puffed up he could rise. He weighs eleven pounds now. He's a blimp. Or maybe a creature from another gravity-laden planet, Jupiter or Uranus.

Someone has explained this to me. This swelling, retention of water, has a logical explanation. The logical explanation is, I forget. I was paying attention but someone sucked out my brains and replaced them with cotton wool. I've been living pure as a nun, no drugs not even Tylenol, and everytime I turn around someone is sticking a needle in my butt and I'm so fuzzy. I was trying to listen. It has something to do with blood pressure. The drugs they are giving him for his blood pressure are causing this? They are giving him a drug to make him swell up so his blood pressure will come down?

Be careful with my outer space baby, my cartoon blimp-boy. Be careful with those needles, if you prick his skin all the air will come out in a low steady hiss and my balloon-baby will fly around the room and deflate and there will be just a withered bit of skin stained with shit I mean meconium lying in the corner of the NICU with the machines going blip-blip-blip and the alarms ringing and the nurses in their blue scrubs.

I am lying in bed. A woman comes into my room.

"Hello. I'm the anesthesiologist. Remember? How are you doing?"

"Not very well."

"Things could be worse."

She's right: my mother's plane could have crashed. Mark could have been hit by a car while crossing the street this morning. I should count my blessings; I should thank my lucky stars.

Maybe she doesn't know.

"My baby might die," I say.

"You're young," she says off-handedly. "You can have another."

"But I love Max," I say. If I shout at her, throw my plastic water pitcher at her, it will only prolong the encounter. I just want her out of my room.

"You have to put on a cheerful face for people around you. You need to take a deep breath every fifteen minutes so you don't get a lung infection," she says. "Can you take a deep breath for me now?"

I take a deep breath for her.

"Good," she says, and leaves the room.

And again that slow shuffle across the hall, to sit in that room filled with warm flat air, and stare at Max's chest moving up and down to the steady in-out of the respirator.

Oh, honey, I'm so sorry. I didn't mean for this to happen. I never would have. I thought you were going to be born at home, with the sunshine pouring in the window and the lilies in the vase on the bureau, a baby who would know just warmth and human touch, nothing cold and metallic.

What a joke.

I didn't have ultrasound and I didn't pump my own gas, I didn't even chew sugarless gum for Christ's sake and now here my son is on phenobarbitol and the other drug that begins with "P" and a bunch of other drugs, too. Right inside the door there are x-rays hanging on the lighted screens. They all say "Boy Finger" along the bottom. There was an article on the front page of the paper just a few weeks ago, saying that most of our knowledge about the effects of x-rays has come from Hiroshima and Nagasaki and scientists are beginning to realize that they have overestimated the amount of radiation that people received there. Thus, routine x-rays may be much more hazardous than previously believed.

Oh, Max, will you hate me? My mother was out to prove to the world that she could be a normal woman, a woman like any other, and I came out crippled with c.p., I came out an epileptic. They had to give me so many x-rays that I got leukemia.

Doctors parade in and out of my room. I deduce the following general principle: the more interventionist and obnoxious the doctor, the thicker the gold chain around his neck.

Harvey does not wear a gold chain at all, he's a regular human being. He tells me to keep taking my pain killers, he tells us to take care of ourselves: get enough sleep, do things for ourselves. (When my friend Lily's son was in intensive care, she was discharged after only two days because she'd had a vaginal birth. She tried to live in the waiting room, which was the only place in the hospital where people could smoke, so everyone went there to smoke. It was like a bar on Saturday night and she was trying to sleep stretched out on the couch till she got sick too.)

Everyone keeps telling me how well I am handling everything, which is a joke too because all I am doing is walking around like a zombie.

That is an alarm going off. The one connected to Max's IV tube goes off every time Mark's camera flashes. There's no day or night in this place, just bright lights always and the damn alarms going off all the time.

My mother and Jane come to the hospital carrying real nightclothes and lemons – so the bland hospital food will have some taste – and lists of friends who have called.

My mother tells me that there was another Max Finger: my father had an Aunt Max, who lived with her sister, Pete, in Brooklyn Heights. They were career girls and they gave my parents a hideous three-footed vase as a wedding present.

"Her name must have been Maxine," my mother said. "I don't know what Aunt Pete's real name was."

I picture two women with stalwart bosoms and mauve hats leaving their brownstone on a January morning and making their way along icy Brooklyn sidewalks to catch the subway. Perhaps Max has a fur coat, not a mink, a beaver, a fur coat that she saved up for years to buy. A sensible fur coat, because a cloth coat is really powerless against snowbelt winters.

"Max," I whisper to my balloon-baby. "There was another Max Finger. My father's aunt. She was a career girl and she lived in Brooklyn. You went with me to Brooklyn before you were born. . . . I thought you were a girl then," I say, which seems funny because I cannot remember why it seemed so important to me to have a daughter.

*

You bloated creature, you shit-stained baby boy, an old derelict with long, raggedy fingernails who they call my son. My mother says she was there when they changed part of his respirator, and he has a beautiful mouth, but I don't believe her. I think there is something wrong with his lip, it's not just the way it looks because the respirator is taped to it, he has an ugly mouth, an ugly mouth, an ugly mouth. This baby is ugly and people are only telling me that he is beautiful so that I won't feel bad. They are telling me he is beautiful because what else can you say about a baby that's paralyzed and taped to a respirator.

"He's such a beautiful baby."

I don't want a beautiful baby. I want a baby that's going to live.

Here is the chaplain, and I haven't got the strength to tell him to go away. He calls me Mrs. Finger, he tells me I have a beautiful baby. He is a kind man: it will be embarrassing if he asks me to pray with him. But he only stays for a minute. He asks me if my son has a name, he likes to be able to use a name when he's praying. So that God won't get confused and help the wrong baby by mistake?

"I'm sure he's going to live," Mark says.

Mark says, "It'll be OK if he has a learning disability."

I'll take epilepsy, or slight but not too severe c.p., as long as he's a genius.

I will be going home soon. The four days allowed for C-section delivery are almost up. I will have to walk through Max's empty room with the bureau that we bought from our next door neighbor Charlie and sanded down and painted, the crib Natalie and Lauren used to sleep in, the receiving blankets, the diapers all folded and waiting, the crib made up, the toys, the clothes. I will have to walk through that nursery that has everything—everything except a baby, into that room where I labored. We could pull out the futon from under the living room couch, I could sleep on that. Except I would still have to walk through the empty room to get to the bathroom.

We are leaving the NICU to sleep. Max's nurse tells us, "I'll let you know if things change during the night." If things change and it looks like your baby is going to stop living, not make it, not pull through.

We stumble back across the hallway to sleep and then shuffle across the corridor, from the room with that awful riot of flowers on the wall, from the hospital room where Mark and I slept with our beds pushed together, holding hands across the gap, breathing together.

This is the sink outside the intensive care unit. Put the yellow robe on. Take a plastic packet down from the box on the shelf above the sink. Scrub your hands. Go through the door with the sign on it that says, "DO NOT USE THIS DOOR." Go past Neda and Christopher. Here is Max, your shit-stained baby boy, your blimp-baby, lying still under the radiant warmer with the electrodes glued to his chest and the respirator taped across his mouth, the tube that says UAC in it running from the black stump of his belly button, the IV line in his foot, the catheter draining urine, his chest moving up and down as the respirator forces air in and out.

14

I kept remembering those battles between life and death in Victorian novels. Oliver Twist returns home to learn that his beloved Rose has fallen into a deep sleep, and from this sleep she will awaken either to recover from her illness and live or to bid them farewell and die. After hours of waiting, the good doctor Losberne comes down and cries passionately, "As He is good and merciful, she will live to bless us all, for years to come."

The word "dying" has disappeared; so has the word "live." Instead, the doctors talk about "making it," "pulling through." Harvey is sitting at the foot of my bed, telling us that Max's condition is improving.

"Is he going to live?" I say.

"It seems that way," he says. "There's always a chance that something else might happen, but if things continue the way they're going now—"

Happiness is impossible. I only feel relief.

See the numbers on this machine? They are going up (or is it down?), they are going in the direction they are meant to be going. Your little lump of flesh is still lying just as he has always lain, under the radiant warmer, with the respirator whooshing air in and out of his lungs and his eyes closed and smeared with artificial tears, but he has turned the corner.

The next morning, Laura hugs me and says, "I finally slept last night." She has lost seven pounds in the past three days.

⸻

They have let you take a shower, wearing a silly little plastic apron with stick-um on the back that protects your scar, your incision that has not yet turned into a scar. Your milk has come in, it was leaking out of your breasts this morning in the shower. Turn on the milking machine, I mean the breast pump, and let the milk get sucked out of you.

You are clean, your baby is going to live, your milk has come in. You are going home. Your baby does not look like a creature from another planet anymore: he peed out six hundred grams last night; he looks almost human. ("Six hundred grams!" the nurse Florrie says. "That's more than some of the babies here weigh.") He has been given his last shot of "the P drug," the one that paralyzes him. They tell us it will be a while before the effects of it wear off.

The fog of numbness that descended when Dr. Holtzmann said, "Yer baby may not liff," has begun to lift. You no longer need what they call denial to keep your heart from stopping.

The four days allowed for a C-section birth have run out. We leave the hospital.

I had forgotten there was a world beyond the narrow shuffle of space between my room and the intensive care unit. The sky! I had forgotten there was a sky.

Mark is about to turn left on Fourth, and I can't figure out why, when I want to go by the ocean. It occurs to me suddenly that he can't read my mind, and I say, "Oh, can you go by the ocean?" I thought he would just know that I wanted to go that way, that our hearts beat the same rhythm and our minds think the same thoughts. He drives another four blocks, and there is Palisades Park, with the homeless people stretched out on the mowed grass beneath the clipped palms and beyond that the ocean. Every now and again I catch a glimpse of the waves breaking, the comforting lap of water against sand.

The *Los Angeles Times* is lying on our dining room table. DEATH TOLL CLIMBS IN MEXICO CITY. I read a few lines. There has been a terrible earthquake days before. I knew nothing about it. The world has kept on turning in my absence.

Now instead of shuffling that distance between my hospital room and the intensive care unit, we drive between the hospital and home, home and the hospital. Market to Main, Main to Pico, Pico to Fourth, take a right on Colorado, a left on Fifteenth. The sliding doors open, take the elevator to the fifth floor, put on a yellow gown, scrub up.

"Max," I say, "this is your mother. I am the person you used to be inside. Remember me? The one who used to say, 'Get up and play, get up and play?'"

We still don't know if, when Max opens his eyes, there will be a blank, unseeing gaze, if a doctor will say in a doleful voice, "His brain damage appears to be quite extensive... ," maybe offering some shred of hope in a dependent clause.

Everyone keeps talking about whether or not Max is going to be "normal." Normal: what an awful word. And how easily they all – we all – use it. I even wrote about it in an article once. With the rise of industrialism, words like "normal" and "defective," words that had once only been used to refer to things, began to be used to refer to people. The shift in language mirrored the shift in belief which mirrored the shift in social reality. In the industrial age, a new degree of uniformity was expected of people. The rhythms and pacing of life could no longer be organic. People became expected to function like things.

When I was in high school in the sixties, my friends and I would have hated to have been called "normal." It was as bad as "typical" or "average." Of course, we meant that we were more, not less: more daring, more free, more radical, more intelligent. Now, when the doctors use it, it means less then normal, not up to snuff.

I have seen bumper stickers that say, "Why Be Normal?" Of course, they mean it in the same way we meant it in high school. But still, I think about getting one of these and putting it on Max's warming table; so that we will all have to ask ourselves, really ask ourselves, that question: Why be normal?

I wake up for my three a.m. feeding. In the absence of a baby to breastfeed, your body will breastfeed the sheets. I am thinking lovingly of my Max, of my lump of flesh whose eyes I will soon see as milk flows out of me. I take another Tylenol with codeine so that I can get back to sleep on the sheets with the damp sticky circles of milk.

Awake again at five-thirty, my breasts are swollen with dammed-up milk, so my mother drives me to the ICU. I stop at the warming table and say, "Honey, I'll be right back," and am rushing over to the breast pump, which is in an alcove behind a curtain, when the respiratory therapist stops me. He is showing me that the numbers on Max's machine have gone from one hundred to thirty: from one hundred per cent oxygen to thirty percent. He is much much better, my little Still Life with Respirator.

I feel as if I am reliving my mother's life. She has talked to me about the guilt she felt because I had polio – guilt that was no less strong for being irrational. She is so soothing to me, telling me, "I talked to Rena Reese – she's working at Meeting Street School now, you know. She said that there are a lot of kids there as a result of birth problems, and they were all born in hospitals." I think, she knows just how I feel, all the guilt, that enormous weight of responsibility, I don't have to say a word.

But later on, when we're having dinner at a fish restaurant near the Santa Monica Pier, my mother says:

"When Max can read, we'll have to get him *Where the Wild Things Are*, because it's about a Max."

I think: don't feed my denial, don't say, "When Max learns to read"; say instead, "If Max learns to read."

It's true: uncertainty is the inner circle of hell. Not to be able to mourn. To have to stop yourself each time you spin dreams about the future. I can't even let myself imagine him taking his first stumbling steps, or let myself wonder what his first word will be.

I decide to let myself believe that Max is going to be capable of having a loving relationship with me. Maybe he will never walk or speak. Maybe he will only smile when I come into the room. Yes, I decide, he will do that – when I come home at the end of a long day, he will smile at the sight of me. It is a big assumption, but nonetheless, I make it. He'll be my child and I'll be his mother.

In the midst of all the turmoil and worry, there is this tiny corner of peace: I have a child I love who will someday love me.

And then one morning when we go in, one of the nurses says that he has opened his eyes. "He seems very alert."

It's odd, the things I remember, the things I don't. I can remember that on Wednesday, the lunch special at the hospital was teriyaki chicken on a sesame seed bun. Yes, and I remember it was that same Wednesday when I sat by mistake at the cafeteria table that seemed to be unofficially reserved for the doctors, sitting there surrounded by men wearing jackets and neckties and eating too fast, crying; crying, and thinking: why am I crying, I should be happy, my child is going to live.

I can remember all that, but I can't remember the first time I saw Max's eyes. That should have been a big dramatic moment. But there's nothing. I do remember holding his hand, and thinking that he might have moved his finger, but it was so slight I really wasn't sure.

I did see my son's blue eyes though. Later on, I would read that in cultures where the infant mortality rate is high, there are social conventions that serve to keep women from becoming too deeply attached to their babies, including warnings against looking into your child's eyes. It is said that then the gods will know how much you love your child, and be jealous, and take him away.

My mother and my sister Jane have both gone home; Jane back to San Francisco, my mother to Rhode Island. I don't remember either of them going, although I know there must have been talk about leaving, arrangements about trips to the airport, goodbyes. I look up and discover they are gone.

When I get to the hospital one day, Max has splints on his hands. One of the nurses, Aurora, explains that he is making a fist with the thumb tucked inside the fingers. This is a brain stem response rather than a cerebral cortex response. The splints will keep him from repeating this negative pattern. I think she is telling me that my son has no functioning cerebral cortex. This frightening piece of information is the most concrete thing we have heard about his condition.

I remember, when I lived in a house on Prospect Street in Cambridge, and my housemates Amy and Wendy worked at a school for the retarded, seeing a few articles that they had about patterning. At the time – nearly ten years previously – it was an alternative therapy for children with severe brain damage; and I remember that it involved hours and hours of intensive therapy, every day, as children were worked through a series of movement exercises which were supposed to resemble the movements babies would make on their own if they weren't brain damaged. The theory was that those patterns would be imprinted on their brains. Supposedly, the brain would then mature and develop normally. The therapy was so intense and time-consuming that volunteers had to be recruited to help with it.

I've seen ads in the paper, once or twice, when I've been reading the classifieds: "Volunteers needed to assist with therapy for brain-damaged child... " I'll have a house filled with do-gooder Christian girls, high school students with scrubbed faces who say, "gee whiz." (When I was your age I was doing every drug I could lay my hands on, what's the matter with you girls?)

But then Laura says that her daughter made a fist with the thumb tucked inside; my friend Peter, with one of the best-developed cerebral cortexes of anyone I know, says he makes his fist with the thumb tucked inside. I notice that when Aurora isn't on duty, the splints are left off.

Max does not have any setbacks. He goes from a respirator to an oxygen tent. We get to hold him, after he and his wires are carefully wrapped up in a blanket by the nurses. Mark takes him in his arms and I hold the tube that pulses oxygen at him. Then he goes from having a cannula delivering oxygen to his nose to breathing what in the hospital is called "room air." He is given a bottle of sterile water at one feeding, then a bottle of half-water, half-expressed breast milk at the next. Then they tell me I can nurse him. Really? So soon?

*

Dr. Holtzmann tells us that Max is localizing pain. When you stick his arm with a needle, he reacts in that arm. This is a good sign, he tells us. How ironic: to be comforted by the thought that my child can feel pain.

The neurologist comes and does an exam. Then she says, "Well, there's nothing *too* alarming."

"What does that mean?"

"Well, I don't see any abnormalities. But it's still pretty early to tell much of anything." Even though I had been told otherwise, I had thought that when the Pavulon wore off and he opened his eyes and could move we would get a diagnosis: your baby has cerebral palsy, he's retarded, he's epileptic.

I have been taught to be not a patient but a health care consumer. Not to be a patient, awaiting the doctor's majesty, but to be an active seeker of services and information, a maker of informed choices. I think that if I start asking some questions I will feel less befuddled. So the next time I see Dr. Holtzmann giving Max a drug I ask him what it is.

"Something that will loosen up the secretions."

"What's the name of it?"

"It's just something that will loosen up the secretions. It gets used a lot for respiratory problems."

"What is it?"

"Something we use all the time."

Finally, when I tell him I have asthma and might know the name of the drug, he tells me aminophylline.

"Oh," I say, "I've taken that."

I remember hearing that anesthesiologists go into that field because they like their patients flat on their back and knocked out. Do neonatologists like the fact that their patients can't talk back—that many premies are too weak even to cry?

*

Finally, Max moves downstairs to a makeshift nursery, where he lies in an ordinary hospital crib like an ordinary baby, swaddled in white hospital blankets. Exactly like an ordinary baby, except for a few leads sticking out from the blanket. They are going to run a test called a pneumogram to see if he is having spells when he is not breathing.

We will be going home in a day or two. "We –" I think that way; we are in the hospital, all three of us. This was what I wanted, having a child, that connection, that root.

I push the playback button on our answering machine and hear my own voice on tape saying, "Hi. Max is still in the hospital but he's doing much better. We really appreciate hearing from all of you and your love and concern. We'll get back to you when we can, but it might be a while." I do not realize how weary I am until I hear my own exhausted voice coming back at me.

"Annie. This is Lily. You have a son just like I do. It sounds like you had some problems. I know what you're going through. Be strong. Congratulations. Call me when you... "

"Hi, Annie. It's Lily again. I forgot to leave you our new phone number... "

"Hi, sweetheart, it's Maggie. Congratulations. I guess your baby is sick, but I'm sure he'll be fine in a day or two... "

"It's Linda again. I'm going to keep calling you every day until I catch you in. Call me when you can. But don't worry, I'll keep calling you. We all love you. Glad to hear Max is doing better."

"Hi, it's Sherry, I talked to Austin. Just wanted to see if there was anything you needed and to give you my best... "

"Hello. This is Ruth. Glad to hear that Max is doing better. We're all praying for you. Give us a call when you can."

The pneumogram shows Max is having apnea spells—he is going as long as twenty seconds without breathing. He needs to come home on an apnea monitor, a device with a belt that fits around his chest and is attached to an electronic box. It will sound an alarm if his heart rate goes too high or too low or if he has an apnea spell.

We have to be trained in CPR, so we can resuscitate Max if he stops breathing. They can't find the English version of the CPR videotape, so they show us the Spanish one, even though neither of us knows Spanish. If Max's alarm goes off we are to shout *Ayuda! Ayuda!* We practice resuscitating a special doll.

It is Wednesday; Max is thirteen days old. We are supposed to leave the hospital today.

I just want to be alone with my baby. I think I know how the people who had sex for Masters and Johnson felt, having their most intimate moments watched. No, this is worse, because I'm not just being watched but critiqued too. I am breastfeeding my baby and a nurse comes up and says, "You're confusing him by holding his head that way." A little while later, another nurse tells me that I should hold him the way I was holding him originally. Another nurse tells me that he could get an infection because I am eating while I am nursing him.

The woman from the home health care company arrives with the monitor. She tells us that when the high heart rate alarm goes off, it's almost always electrical interference. Do you live in an apartment, do you have a computer? Both of those can cause an electrical disturbance. Here is a stethoscope. We practice using it so that we can check his heart rate, to be sure the machine is right.

There is something wrong with the first monitor; no

matter what the woman does, the machine won't pick up Max's respirations. So we have to wait while another monitor is brought from the office. "I hope we can sort this out," she is saying, "so you can go home today after all."

I think, maybe we could go home without the monitor if we promised the hospital that we would keep watch over him all night, sleep in shifts, and then get the apnea monitor tomorrow. I just want to be alone with my baby.

At last the monitor arrives. It's hooked up, yes it works, we are going, we are going, we are going at last.

Not quite. Suddenly one of the nurses leaps in front of us with a form. You're planning to breastfeed? Do you feel that all your questions about breastfeeding have been adequately addressed? Are you going to supplement? Would you like to take home some samples of Enfamil just in case? Do you know how to change diapers? Do you feel comfortable dressing the baby? Ah, no one has demonstrated how to give a baby a bath.

That's all right, I say, I can figure it out.

Are you sure? It won't take more than five or ten minutes. Yes, I am sure, I am sure, I am sure.

I am sure that I want to be alone. When we get back home, we go into the back bedroom and I take off my shirt and sit on the bed where Max was meant to be born, nursing my Max, in the room with the redwood paneling, with the late afternoon sun coming in through the window. The lilies are dead in their vases on the bureau. For the past week, I have been telling myself that I have to dump those damn things in the garbage, but I never seem to have a minute.

Our childbirth educator told us that breastfed babies needed to be fed about every two hours, and that you could plan on spending half an hour to an hour nursing each time. I thought: that can't be right. Or maybe I thought—not my baby. But she was right, mostly I am nursing, letting the milk flow out from my breasts into his mouth. This is my baby: I have made him and I am making him still.

I see why they want to cover this up, make infancy a time of inanity, of lambies and duckies and bunnies, a Hallmark greeting card world. There is nothing cutesie-pie about this: this pure fit of your body against mine, this naked way we make him child and he makes us parents.

We could sit for hours and watch that ever-changing face. The brow wrinkles as if in worry, a flicker of a smile, the lips purse and relax. What are you dreaming of? Where were you before you were here? Nowhere? How is that possible? I ask myself again all those foolish questions I haven't asked since I was nine, ten years old.

We go to see our pediatrician, Harvey, a week after we leave the hospital. He asks us whether we have smoke detectors and a car seat; he tells us to give Max a bottle of expressed breastmilk or diluted juice every other day or so, so that he'll stay used to a bottle. We don't need to worry about sterilizing the bottles, but we should boil the rubber nipples several times to leach out chemicals. This is what he says to all his patients. We are regular parents.

15

Fighting my way up from sleep. An alarm beeping at me. I'm so tired, I just want to. Beep. Beep. Beep. Can't Mark wake up and. Beep. Beep.

It is his high heart rate alarm. It's four-thirty in the morning. Remember, the woman from the monitor company said that if the high heart rate alarm went off it would probably be caused by electrical interference. Mark gets the stethoscope. "His heart is really racing."

Is this really an emergency? Who should we call? First we call the monitor people, who have told us they have a twenty-four hour answering service. Mark lets the phone ring twenty or thirty times but there's no answer. We call the ICU – at least we won't be waking anybody up. They tell us to call Harvey, who tells us to drive around for fifteen or twenty minutes and see if that brings his heart rate down. If not, we should call him back and he'll meet us at his office.

Yesterday's clothes pulled out of the hamper. My cotton Japanese jacket, my pink and white cloth shoes. Grab the diaper bag; grab the two bananas that are all the fruit that's in the fruit bowl. Drive around, Harvey said, and without thinking we are taking our old familiar route, Market to Main to Pico, left on Fourth, right on Colorado, as if we were driving to Santa Monica Hospital. It's still really racing, Mark says. We stop at a public phone. It's five-thirty a.m., I'm shivering in the open phone booth. Yes, I tell the woman at the answering service, this is an emergency.

Being out so early in the morning usually makes me feel like I'm back in high school – waiting, maybe, in a grassy park early in the morning for buses that will take us to a demonstration in New York or Washington; or maybe high on acid wandering the streets after having been thrown out of the Hungry Sheik when it closed at two. I was never dressed warmly enough, my feet always hurt –

But now I don't feel seventeen; I feel thirty-three, a solid thirty-three.

"You're out in Topanga?" Harvey is saying.

"No." I almost say, we don't live in Topanga, we live in Venice. "At a phone booth in Santa Monica."

We meet Harvey at his office. I can smell garlic on his breath. He borrows Mark's watch; he has forgotten his own.

Harvey says, "This is not serious." We do not have to worry about losing him, about him not pulling through. We need to go to UCLA Hospital, that's where they have the best cardiology department. "What they'll probably do is admit him to the pediatric ICU for a day."

I am crying when we leave his office. I didn't think that we would have to go through this again, rubber-soled shoes squeaking against linoleum hospital floors, sleeping stretched out on a couch with a scrounged thermal blanket tucked around me, holding Mark's hand across the gap between our makeshift beds: Max in the hospital again. Religious preference? none; "Hey, Mark, what's your social security number?"; getting lost in the hospital corridors, having to ask, "Which way is it to the ICU?"; holding Max while in the background monitors beep and alarms go off.

Having to repeat the litany for doctor after doctor: severe fetal distress, asphyxia, meconium aspiration, Apgars of 1, 4 and 5, thirteen days in the ICU, on a respirator, Pavulon. Now he's just taking phenobarbital.

"Is this Baby Finger?"

"Yes; Max."

"I'm Dr. Hill. I'm a resident in pediatrics. Dr. Karp called." She's a big woman in blue scrubs, a laminated plastic ID card clipped to her collar. She writes notes on a white three-by-five index card.

I hardly cried at all last time. Now I am sitting in the corner, sobbing. When he was in the hospital last time I had my numbness to protect me, and then my sense of relief. Now this trip back terrifies me: is this what our lives are going to be like now – alarms in the middle of the night, journeys to hospitals, having to stand by helplessly and watch while pain is inflicted on my child?

The resident leaves. A nurse comes in and weighs him, takes his vitals, making a note of his blood pressure and pulse in pencil on the bedsheet. She tries to do an EKG with a regular machine, designed for adults, but the suction cups keep popping off his chest.

"This is ridiculous," she says, while Max wails. "We're never going to get a decent reading with this thing." Well, then just stop it for Christ's sake; get the right-sized machine; he's been through enough all ready.

"You have a problem with hypertension and diabetes, do you have any other medical problems?" someone is shouting at another patient, hidden behind a curtain. "How old are you?"

"Eighty-three."

"Max," I say, "that man is eighty-three. You're three weeks old, and that man is eighty-three years old."

A resident in cardiology comes down to the emergency room.

"What I'm going to do," he says, "is put an ice bag over your baby's face, hold it there for thirty seconds. With an older person, we can tell them to hold their breath and push, like they're having a bowel movement... Sometimes that'll get the heart rate to come down." He puts the ice bag over Max's face three times.

"I didn't think it would work," he says. "Usually it doesn't, but it's worth a try."

An x-ray. "One of you will have to stay in here with him," the tech says, "to hold his arms up."

"You do it," I say to Mark. "I've had enough x-rays."

Mark joins me on the bench outside, with Max in his arms screaming. "It's a good thing you weren't in there; it was pretty awful."

Another EKG, the needle darting across the graph paper.

It's ten in the morning. The cafeteria has just closed, so Mark goes to the vending machines and returns with a Buttermilk Twizzle and a package of Hostess Donettes, two half-pint containers of orange juice.

"The other stuff was worse," he says.

"You'd think if it was this bad for you, it would at least taste good... how can they ruin orange juice?"

Nursing Max and crying. They need to draw blood, they need to get an IV line in him, never an easy task with a baby's tiny veins.

"Do you mind if we try his scalp?"

"If that's easiest."

Dr. Hill lays gauze pads, syringes, rubber bands, tubes and a razor on the bed.

"They're going to have to shave his head," I say, nodding to the razor.

"I'm going to put a rubber band around his head," the doctor says. "It'll make his veins stand out." Max's eyes look up at us, me and Mark, begging.

"Oh, Max," I say. "I know you don't like this. I know. I know." A murmur against his cries. "I know. I know. I

160

know." Licking my little finger and putting it in his mouth, stroking the roof of his mouth while he sobs between sucks.

The doctor taps her finger against his flesh until a vein appears; she shaves a patch of his scalp; the needle goes in, but not into the vein, and she probes, pulling the needle in and out, in and out, in and out, while he wails in pain. He stares into my eyes and I cry with him, wanting to say, "It's not me that's doing this to you."

"Oh, Max," I say. "I'm sorry, I'm sorry, I'm so sorry."

Between tries they let me comfort him, buttoning and unbuttoning my shirt, unsnapping and resnapping my nursing bra.

"Did you get it?"

"Did you get it?"

They shave the other side of his head. More doctors come down from the pediatric intensive care unit to have a turn trying to get the needle into his vein. The rubber band comes off his head; a blood pressure cuff goes around his arm so they can try the veins there.

I close my eyes and cry with Max; I visualize his blood running up into the tube. I keep opening my eyes to the sight of the clear, bloodless line. Finally, one time, I open my eyes and there it is, they've gotten the line in.

"There you go, Maxie. They got it. They got it. They're not going to stick you anymore."

Taping his arm to a splint. Heparin flush and then a drug with a name that sounds like dioxin.

"This drug should bring his heart rate down. It may not, and then we'll try administering an electrical shock to the heart. You've probably seen it done on TV," one of the doctors says.

"On *Dr. Kildare*," someone else says.

We all parade up, Max and Mark and an entourage of doctors and me, to the peds intensive care unit.

Max is hungry, but they won't let me feed him. They're afraid he might vomit and choke if they have to shock his heart. I lick my little finger and stick it into his dry mouth, letting him suck on that.

A man appears to do another EKG. He attaches the leads to Max as if he were an inanimate object, flopping his limbs this way and that while I whisper to him, "Hey, Max, it's OK. They're just doing an EKG. They're not going to stick any more needles into you." Max is screaming.

"Bag it," I hear from the table where the doctors are. The attending physician comes up and says to the EKG tech, "I know you were asked to come up here, but we got a pretty good reading and right now we just want to get him calmed down. So we're going to bag it. Mom, why don't you hold him. Can you turn down the lights?" he calls to one of the nurses.

"Leave the leg leads on, we'll use them to monitor."

I hold Max in my arms. The monitor is flashing his heart rate: 136 – 124 – 130.

"I guess that drug worked," I say to the doctor.

"It's probably double that." He comes over and puts a stethoscope against Max's heart. "Yeah, the machine's dividing it in half." At least it looks impressive, with that wavering blue line and that constantly changing readout.

Finally the cardiologist arrives. Max's heart is still racing, five hours is a long time to be in this state, they're going to give a shock to his heart. The cardiologist says, "Madam, would you please wait outside."

Don't call me Madam. My name is Anne. I'm just a kid of thirty-three. I should have insisted on staying. But I'm glad too to be outside the door, not to have to watch.

The door opens and I hear the sound of Max crying. We can come in, I can nurse him, his heart rate has gone down. You might notice two marks on his chest, like burn marks, nothing to be concerned about.

They're going to keep him here for twenty-four hours, just to keep an eye on things. We'll be going home tomorrow morning; Max will keep taking the drug I call dioxin. I call it dioxin even though I know it's not called that, even though I know dioxin is the name of a horrible cancer-causing chemical.

I nurse Max. "It's all over, sweetie. They had to do that to you. It's all right now."

There is a television hanging from the ceiling above each of the beds. I see a television commercial for Forest Lawn Cemetery. A not-quite-old woman is sitting on beautifully tended grass, with a fountain and a Grecian temple in the background. "If only my husband had known... " she says. She is The Deceased. She is telling the audience that she would have been much happier buried at Forest Lawn than in the cramped graveyard her husband has consigned her to.

Another girl of two or three is admitted. She starts screaming as soon as anyone with a stethoscope comes near her. I think that she must have cancer.

"Show the nurse what a good girl you can be," her father says.

Fuck you, I think. She's been through enough, don't tell her she has to be a good girl, too, don't tell her not to cry.

I have never been this tired before. I lie down in the waiting area. Someone is watching a football game. Two suitcases are tucked in a corner, with an iron and a blow dryer on top of them. It turns out that they belong to the family of Maria, the Latina girl in the bed next to Max, who has had a kidney transplant. They have come from Bakersfield to be with her, and they have set up camp in this waiting room.

When I was a kid in the hospital, visiting hours were twice a day, an hour long. Now, they let parents visit all day long. They even provide cots for us to sleep on.

Mary, Max's nurse, is showing us where the cots are. She explains that there aren't enough to go around, and parents get in arguments over them. We should grab these two now. She writes a note and tapes it onto the cots. "RESERVED FOR PARENTS OF BABY IN ICU. MAX FINGER."

We go home for a while, to get some food and a nightgown and bathrobe. I record a new message on the answering machine: "We're back in the hospital again."

Later, someone comes and takes one of the cots: the rule is one narrow cot per patient. I set up my cot in the art therapy room. When I unfold it, I see that the center leg is shorter than the legs on either end, so it dips down into the middle in a "V" shape. How did they ever manage to find something so uncomfortable? Was it a manufacturing error, and UCLA got them at a ninety percent discount?

From the waiting room, you can see the Medstar helicopter with all its fancy machines and equipment, landing and taking off from the roof.

Another boy is brought into the peds ICU, a two-year-old who is waiting for a liver transplant. He is put in a crib at the far end of the enormous room. A few other patients have been moved out of the ICU to make room for him. I hope that the doctors will decide to move Max out, but they don't. A doctor shakes his head and says, "Boy, we almost lost him there in the ER."

Mark goes home to sleep; I fall asleep on my V-shaped cot. The nurses come down to wake me up so I can nurse. Every two hours I am padding down the hall in my slippers and bathrobe. Throughout the night, the doctors and nurses are huddled around the crib at the far end.

When I am led down for the four a.m. feeding, there are only two names on the list of patients outside the door, Max and the girl who had the kidney transplant. I hear myself say to the nurse, "That little boy, he didn't make it?"

Max did come home the next day. I kept wondering what was going to go wrong next. When he coughed I thought he had pneumonia, when his lip trembled I worried it might be a seizure. Pneumonia, seizures, we'd been warned about them; but the heart problem had been totally unexpected. Suppose his kidneys started to malfunction, suppose some other body system suddenly went haywire on us?

Maybe only things I *hadn't* worried about were going to go wrong, so perhaps I could keep him safe if I worried about everything, always.

Five

16

I do worry. I worry about the things that have gone wrong and the things that might go wrong. I worry religiously, as if my worrying could protect him; as if the things I imagine will never come true.

On my birthday a few weeks after Max was born, Mark and I go out for dinner. Our friend Michelle who has been trained in CPR is staying with Max; I leave a single-spaced typed sheet of Max's medical history. I sit there in the Indian restaurant and imagine blood suddenly spurting from the middle of Max's back. I keep seeing it over and over and over again, a red fountain of blood jetting from him.

And I cry every day. I cry over the loss of the beautiful birth I had hoped to have. I cry over the loss of the dream of the perfect child, of the perfect parent I had hoped to be.

But I have never been happier.

I love this physical connection: your mouth on my breast, your unceasing stare at my face, the wiping away of drool and spit-up and shit; the way I kiss your feet, the insides of your elbows, your thighs. You are me and not me. We are one and yet two. This is what I have been waiting for, maybe since my own infancy. I am not alone anymore.

But you are my dictator, too, my ten-pound tyrant. Your crying makes me frantic. I jiggle you up and down;

when that doesn't work, I climb onto the Amigo and go back and forth, dining room to living room and then back again, which comforts you. As long as I keep moving.

In my other life, my life before you were born, I took for granted being able to make a cup of coffee, go to the bathroom. Now everything gets interrupted. In the kitchen I find half-made cups of coffee gone cold. I have to pee but I'm nursing. You fall asleep and I rush to take advantage of it, return a phone call. Halfway through the conversation I realize I *have* to go to the bathroom, and say: "Can you hold on for just a minute?"

I read an article, a psychoanalytically-based interpretation of psycho-sexual development, explaining how some people seek to replicate the mother-infant relationship in their sexual relationships, seeking to be the all-powerful mother or the dependent infant. No, I think, the author's got it backwards: it's the infant who's all-powerful, the mother who is helpless.

We go back to visit the ICU at Santa Monica Hospital one night. As we are getting back into our car, two teenage boys emerge from behind the corner of the hospital. They are rowdy enough that for a second my city-ingrained wariness switches on. Then I realize that one of them is saying:

"I am a fucking father, man."

"Yeah," his friend answers.

"I am a fucking *father*."

"Hey, man."

"I am going to be a hard-working father. My kid is not going to be on welfare. I am going to have to work hard. I am going to be a ha-ard-working father, man. . . . " I listen to him shout exultantly into the night, and listen while his voice fades as he swaggers past the hospital and on down Fifteenth Street.

I listen to his voice fade, and I feel so cheated that we never got that moment of pure joy, that we never got to shout foolish promises into the night sky.

At times my fear becomes sharp, a pang: my son may be retarded. I feel panicky, desperate, overwhelmed by the sense that there is nothing I can do. Nothing. My son may be retarded and it doesn't matter what I do, how hard I try, it is beyond my control.

When I was growing up, I was expected to live not in my body but in my mind. I was supposed to be smart and I was smart. In fourth grade, when we were assigning parts for the school play the teacher said, "Who would like to be the announcer?" and I knew that I was supposed to raise my hand, and I did. The teacher smiled and said, "Anne, you know, I pictured you as the announcer." I was supposed to be outside the action, the observer, the one who explained. I was good at that role. Perhaps that is why I became a writer. Now I have a son who may be retarded. His body now is almost flawless; after all he went through, there's just one tiny scar on his chest, where they inserted the tube after his lung collapsed. But he may not be able to think the way that I can think. He may not be able to do the thing that I've built my life around.

I have to make myself face the fear: well, what of it? He can still have a good life. He can still be happy. What am I afraid of? Of my own sense of guilt, my feeling that I am responsible. Of my feeling of shame: people will stare at us in the street, I will be even more of an oddity than I am now. Of having to confront my own obsession with intellect. When I face my fear, really face it, it melts away.

And still, I imagine our future. I see him, limping along next to me, me leaning on my cane and rolling my whole body up to throw my right leg ahead, while he walks next to me, with the jerky, lumbering gait of a spastic. A spastic. A cripple. Or worse: a retard. I have thoughts that would not be approved by *Disability Rag*.

I understand all this very well, I understand that under capitalism, the concept of normalcy is used to reinforce the standardization necessary for industrial culture. That children are seen as possessions, commodities. While in my head it repeats like a chant: I don't want anything to be wrong with him, I don't want anything to be wrong with him, I don't want anything to be wrong with him. And that sits side by side with my knowledge that I will love him no matter what.

My friend Vicky says, "We need to build a disabled culture because we've been so trained to hate ourselves that we hate each other." My knowledge of that truth sits side by side in my heart with the steady beat that says, "I don't want to have a retarded child. I don't want to have a retarded child. I don't want to have a retarded child."

Did I think because I stand up on platforms and make speeches about disability rights, did I think because I know so much that I was exempt from feelings of self-hatred? Did I think because I can talk about it with big words, "internalized oppression," "human diversity and inter-dependence," did I think that because I understand so much that I was exempt from the hurt?

I know there's pain in everyone's life—but I know the pain of disability so well. The old feelings surface: can't I have a new struggle? I'm sick of this one. Will I have to relive through him the world of stares and loneliness and shame? Of hospitalizations, cold stethoscopes against a warm chest, waking in the night alone in a metal bed?

I wanted something perfect to come out of my body. All my life I've had to fight for everything. Walking across a room is work. I wanted something to just happen. I wanted something not to be hard. Other people have babies and all they have to deal with is diaper rash and sleepless nights.

In those first weeks I found that I had to relive, again and again, all my experiences. At first my labor itself had been impossible to remember, because every time I thought about it, I felt such a wash of guilt and sadness. Bit by bit, a fragment here, a fragment there, my memories came back to me: how I labored all night and all day and into the next evening in our back bedroom. Throwing up the glass of orange juice into the metal pan. Jane sitting quietly in the rocking chair.

Then I remembered the trip to the hospital. I had to get back every detail: I wore my grey dress and a nursing bra and my run-down running shoes and I had a contraction just after we had turned onto Colorado from Fourth. For a long time I could remember looking over to Laura and saying, "Is this all right?" but couldn't remember Dr. Resnick telling me I needed a C-section. Then it came back to me, the short man with the gold chain around his neck, bending over me and saying, "You can wait until Dr. Garnett gets here and he'll do a C-section or we can do one right now."

I had to imagine too what it would have been like if Max had died. I saw myself walking into the photo store; lowering my voice as I hand the roll of film to the clerk: "My baby died, and these are the only pictures I have of him. So please be very, very careful when you develop them."

I saw myself standing in a windy BART station back in San Francisco, waiting for the train. Someone I know is standing on the opposite platform. She sees me and hollers across the tracks: "Anne! Hi! Did you have a boy or a girl?" And there I stand, a lump rising in my throat, while the figure on the opposite side of the tracks cups her hand around her mouth and shouts again, "A boy or a girl?" her voice wavering a little in the wind. I can't shout back, "My baby died," can't shout those words in the crowded BART station, can't shout them loudly enough to be heard above the wind and the rumbling of the escalators and a train on another track. But calling back "A boy" seems like a lie.

I imagined a memorial service for him, held at a book-store in San Francisco, reading the death carol from Walt Whitman's "When Lilacs Last in the Dooryard Bloomed."

Every day, for weeks and weeks, I remembered those things that never happened: saying to the woman behind the counter in the photo store, "My baby died and these are the only pictures we have of him"; standing in the windy BART station, while some acquaintance shouts across the platform, "Did you have a boy or a girl?" and I stand silent, not knowing what to say. Looking around at all the faces at the memorial service, and hearing my voice cracking as I read, "Come, lovely and soothing Death... "

I suppose it's like having a bad fright: someone startles you and your heart keeps pounding and you keep shaking long after you realize it is just your roommate coming up the stairs, not an axe murderer.

They tell me to talk to you, that it's important for you to be out in the world, not lying in your crib. The infant brain is plastic, it's important for you to have stimulation. So I talk and I talk, about the vegetables when I am peeling vegetables, about the other cars when I am driving on the freeway. I sing you songs, "Love Me, I'm a Liberal," "This Little Light of Mine"; I sing you old Wobblie songs, "Pie in the Sky," and "Farther along, we'll get off their wages; farther along we'll get off of their pay.... " I sing: "O would you from hunger and misery be free, than come do your share like a person.... " My mother said the reason that none of us could carry a tune was that she sang to us in her off-key voice when we were babies.

A loud noise makes you throw out your arms, a monkey grasping for his monkey-mother at the sound of danger. You are my little baboon. You are humanity's past.

This flinging-out of arms is called a startle reflex. It is one of a number of reflexes that are present in early infancy but which usually fade within days or weeks. Yours is not fading as it should. This persistence of your startle reflex is of "some concern" but "nothing to be alarmed about," they say. (Do doctors ever say, "This is something to be alarmed about"?) We must remember about the plasticity of the human brain. We must remember that there are children born with a condition called "transilluminance": shine a light behind their heads and the light shines clear through. There's just a smattering of brain cells on the top of their skulls. Yet some of them function normally. Some of them.

Harvey says your reflexes are a little brisk. What does that mean? I ask. It's still too early to tell, he says.

This is the dance I do with doctors these days. I am told something about you is abnormal. When I ask what that portends for the future, they say they really have no idea. The alternative, of course, is for them not to tell me what they see. I guess this is better.

Did anyone ever read infant development charts the way that I did? Before Max was born, I'd borrowed a slew of standard infant care and development books from my well-prepared friend Austin. In the back of one, scarcely noticed before you were born, were developmental charts, outlining normal development month by month. There was a warning printed at the bottom of each one: "THESE CHARTS ARE TO BE USED AS A GUIDE ONLY. NORMAL INFANT DEVELOPMENT VARIES."

I sneaked looks at them the way I used to sneak looks at *Playboy* magazines when I was a kid – with that same mix of guilt and fascination. I would keep telling myself, don't look, don't obsess about this, it's a guide, it's not meant to be. . . . It says that at six months of age the noises a baby makes are beginning to resemble speech. Am I kidding myself that those earnest "babababababas" are his attempt at conversation? Or am I so worried that my fears prevent me from seeing what is in front of my face? When they say at seven months, do they mean at the beginning of the seventh month or the end?

I never wanted to be one of those watchful, hawk-like mothers, looking for faults and lags in other children, measuring them against her own. But when David smiles before Max, I feel heartsick. And when Max Rosen can point at the pictures in the farm animals book and say "Baabaa" at the sheep and "Moo-moo" at the cow, I want to cry. And when my Max can do something better than a kid his own age, I gloat.

Slowly I start to write this book – at first just putting words on a page for myself. I spend all of one morning trying to write, Max in one arm, my free hand ranging over the keys, and I get all of four words written. Still, I tell myself, you got those four words down.

It comes back to me in fragments: a word here, a phrase someone said there. I hopscotch around on the screen of my word processor; I jot words and phrases in my big orange notebook.

Sometimes, at the end of the day Mark would come home and I would run out to a coffeehouse to write, run out with just my pen and notebook and wallet and keys, feeling impossibly light. I'm gliding on air, not weighted down with diaper bag and stroller and spare outfit and apnea monitor and baby. I run out with my pen and notebook. No one knows I'm a mother. I feel like an imposter.

Motherhood is physical pain. Mostly a vague ache everywhere and exhaustion. But when I stand up after sitting down for a while, the first few steps are like walking on broken glass, except the broken glass is inside my ankle. Sometimes I can't help it, I put my foot down and cry out in pain. If I have to get up to take a leak in the middle of the night, I crawl to the bathroom so I won't feel those shards of pain shooting through my joint.

Motherhood is exhaustion, and feeling helpless. My house will never be clean, or when it is clean, it will stay that way for ten minutes and milk is leaking out of my breasts onto my sheets, onto my shirts, and my desk is piled, and the sink is piled and I do a load of diapers and the hot water hits the shit and piss and that stink mixes with the smell of the pink perfumed laundry detergent and rises into the air.

It's the *slowness* that I notice most. I walk at half the pace most people do (except when I'm tired, then I'm even slower). That means that almost every household chore – going shopping, picking up things around the house – takes at least twice as long. (Except when I'm tired, which is always these days, then it takes three times as long.)

Someone shows me a quote from an eminent psychologist, saying that the real work of parenting is not physical but emotional. I think: this man never nursed a baby, never washed dirty diapers, never lifted a baby in and out of a crib twenty times a day with an aching back. He means, I suppose, that it isn't only a physical process, that there's a lot more to it. But especially in infancy the physical is intertwined with the emotional. Love grows out of the work, out of the endless rocking, out of the sleeplessness; it grows from the physical root.

I've never worked harder, never in my life. When Max falls asleep, I don't dawdle, I go straight to the computer and turn it on, and then pee while it is loading, I save a whole minute that way. I get up early in the morning and write looking out at the window as the sky turns from night-black to grey to blue; I listen for the thump of the newspapers landing on porches up the street as the delivery man in his dirty white truck cruises slowly up Market Street, tossing them from the window. Sometimes I sit you in your infant chair on my desk and talk to you about what I am writing.

I am a mother and the world is made new: a wound raw and open. I can't read the newspaper anymore without crying. The pictures of starving women in Ethiopia, a baby on each hip, are *real*, I think every time I look at them. These are women who love their children as I love Max.

Motherhood is this river of love, a door into the world without clock-time, it is the world cracked open and made new and it is this physical ache, the weariness seeping out from my bones, this dopey haze of love.

They took out the staples they used to repair my incision four days after the surgery. It didn't seem possible that my body could have healed so quickly when the grief I felt as a result of my having had a C-section was just beginning to surface.

Sometimes I think that the very necessity of the C-section was what made it so hard for me. It wasn't that the doctors bamboozled me, it wasn't that I could have done it and I just didn't give myself a chance – I just couldn't give birth to my son.

I have a child, and still, I have never seen a child being born.

I didn't want another scar. I don't care if it's bright purple and thick or if it fades and I'll never see it again. I didn't want another scar and I don't care if it is a bikini scar and it's covered by my pubic hair and no one will ever notice it. I still know it's there.

Almost as soon as we knew that Max was going to live, I started to fantasize about having another child. When I went into bookstores I would go first of all to the childbirth section, like I did when I was first pregnant. I would imagine again a perfect birth, seeing our back bedroom with the redwood panelling and me pushing, and pushing, and Mark holding me. I felt it all: I feel like I'm shitting and it's my baby. And then the sensation of being split in half, and the burning, and I push again, and the head crowns and I push again and the head is born, and then my child comes into the world. I know I am focusing on the next birth as a way not to think about the pain of this one: wanting to rush into the future rather than deal with the past.

When I would get on the freeway or into the bathtub, and my mind was no longer busy, I would start crying. Sometimes I would find my body pushing as I cruised down the Santa Monica Freeway or as I lay back in the bathtub: trying to do again what I could not do before. Sometimes I even imagined that there was another baby inside, Max's twin, not yet born, and that if I would just keep pushing he would come out, with a mottled face and a molded head, the way a real baby looks.

When Max is four months old, I am invited to speak at the Women and the Law conference in Chicago. It's a national conference of women lawyers and law students that's been meeting annually since the late sixties. I've spoken at their conferences a few times before, on disability rights, reproductive rights, some combination of the two.

I am so glad to be going. When the plane lifts off the runway, it's as thrilling as the first time I ever flew. I'm in the air! This is who I used to be. I haven't lost my life. As I get off the plane, I remember a Spanish phrase my friend Susan used, when I was carrying too many things: *bien encargada*. Yes, I am *bien encargada* now, diaper bag and apnea monitor, digoxin and phenobarbitol tucked in my briefcase with my papers.

We stay in the hotel where the conference is held. The bathroom is all mirrors. It seems like such an odd design: when you sit on the toilet you get met by the reflection of yourself, sitting on the toilet.

And when I climb out of the bathtub, there is my new body, wet and naked. It is the first time I have really had to look at myself, naked and whole, since Max was born. I want to close my eyes. Silvery stretch marks are etched into my belly, a pouch of flesh hangs above the scar – a C-section leaves you with a pouch, plus my abdominal muscles are weak, they don't tighten up again like most women's would after a pregnancy. The purple scar itself is faintly visible behind my pubic hair. I hate my body from the waist down.

My body is split in half: the good and the bad. After all, that was what I always heard as a child, and not just from doctors and physical therapists. My left leg was my good leg, my right leg was my bad leg. I jump now when I hear someone say "good leg," or "bad leg," it's like the word "cripple" or "deformed"; but I know that language has dug its way into my bones.

It used to be that the bad part of my body ended at the top of my legs. Now, it's crept upward; the bad part of my body has reached my navel. It's bad because it's ugly, because it doesn't look the way a body is supposed to look, because the doctors have written on it. It's true, I don't experience my body as me; sometimes I don't even experience it as belonging to me; it seems that it belongs to the medical world.

It's hard enough to make myself see again the way I looked that day as I climbed out of the bathtub, surrounded by reflected images of my changed body. It's harder still to write about it. I promised myself once that I would never again say anything about self-hatred, except to other disabled people. The first time I ever spoke on a panel as a disabled person, I talked in part about my journey from self-hatred, from rejecting others who were disabled to finding community. The next day, I read a newspaper account of my talk: the only things reported were the negative things I had said. I said to myself then, don't ever tell the whole truth, not to them. If you do, they will take the fragment of that truth that they want to hear and not hear anything else. The self-hatred is what they want to hear, it's the only thing they will hear.

At the conference, I go to a panel on court-ordered C-sections. A woman who is an ob/gyn resident at a Chicago hospital tells this story: A Nigerian woman living in Chicago was pregnant with triplets. Because a multiple pregnancy is a high-risk pregnancy, she was admitted to the hospital six weeks before her due date. The doctors told her that she would have to have a C-section – because of the multiple pregnancy, and because the first child was breech. Both the woman and her husband had strong religious and cultural objections to having a Cesarean and told the doctors that under no circumstances did they want the children delivered surgically. The doctors made plans that as soon as she went into labor, they would call the district attorney's office and attempt to get a juvenile court judge to issue an emergency order for a Cesarean. They did not inform the couple of their plans.

The woman went into labor. The judge was told that without the C-section, the woman and her babies would die. (Although multiple births are certainly riskier than single ones, they are hardly likely to be fatal for either mother or child.) An order for an emergency C-section was granted. It took seven security guards to drag the protesting husband from the hospital. The woman was bound hand and foot before she was anesthetized, and her three babies were cut from her. All recovered from the birth. A few months later, the husband committed suicide.

I keep seeing the woman being bound hand and foot in

the leather restraints, the security guards wrestling with the man. I can see his black skin glistening with perspiration, I can see the seven security guards. Most of them are Black too. One of them is trying to talk to him as they drag him down the hospital corridor. They are moving him towards the freight elevator, trying to stop the other patients from hearing him scream. One of the guards is saying to him, "Hey, you're just making it harder on yourself, man. Come on. Come on."

I see the woman, her eyes flashing in fear, struggling as they wrap the restraints around her wrist and legs. This cannot be happening. She has said no, and yet they are tying her to a table and they are going to cut her open. She has said no, and yet she is powerless to stop them.

This is not an isolated incident. More and more, doctors are convincing judges to order women to undergo C-sections. This is a dangerous assault on women's bodily autonomy. There are no other circumstances where a competent adult will be ordered to undergo surgery, even if the surgery will save that person's life, or, in the case of a kidney or bone marrow transplant, save someone else's life. It is a frightening extension of medical and social control over women's bodies. In several cases women have fled after being ordered by courts to undergo C-sections. So far, in every case where women have done this, they have delivered healthy children vaginally. This was after doctors convinced judges that a vaginal birth would be almost inevitably fatal to the fetus.

On a personal level, the whole notion of extending medical control over women terrifies me: I could be made a child again, subject to the whims of gods with knives.

Those first few months after Max was born, when I was wading through that morass of grief and joy and nights of broken sleep, those first few months when I was still crying every time I drove on the freeway or got into the bathtub, I kept thinking about how what you need to deal with will always return to you.

Here is another scar, when you already have so many scars. There is no way out: you live in the prison of this body. Disabled people are supposed to overcome our bodies, not be them. I wanted to be my body, wanted to go where it had to go, without the doctors, without their scalpels. But I couldn't.

History repeats itself, as tragedy and as farce. I never wanted to have to deal with the disability bureaucracy again, and now I found myself more locked into them than ever.

I am trying to get help from California Children Service (formerly Crippled Children's Services), a bureaucracy of astonishing impenetrability.

I talk to one of the social workers on the phone: "No, you don't want to talk to us. You're not showing up as eligible, so you want to talk to Eligibility."

I am transferred to Eligibility; no, I've just had my eligibility review, I need to get transferred back to the social workers, who promptly transfer me back to Eligibility, who...

"Listen, there's obviously some sort of a problem here. Isn't there someone who can help straighten this out, a worker who's assigned to me?"

"No, we have a team approach."

"But Eligibility says I'm eligible and you say I'm not."

"You need to speak to Eligibility. I'll transfer you."

"No, please," I call into the telephone, "don't transfer me."

Another call to CCS:

"There's a map that came with your letter—" the voice on the other end of the phone is saying.

"No, I didn't get a map with my letter."

"Then you didn't get a letter from us."

"Yes," I say, "I did get a letter from you, but it didn't have a map with it."

"If you had got a letter from us, it would have had a map in it."

"I have the letter right here in my hand. It says California Children Services on the top. But there's no map with it."

"OK. There's a map that came with it."

"No, there isn't."

"Then you didn't get a letter from us."

"I did fucking so get a goddamn letter from you." The phone clicks dead. "I did so get a goddamn letter from you," I scream into the blank receiver and start to cry.

Perhaps in a previous life I was a bureaucrat, a particularly nasty and officious bureaucrat who was always away from my desk, who never returned calls, who never smiled at a client, who could recite chapter and verse a byzantine code of procedures and who always lost my clients' paperwork.

Finally, I wrote a letter to CCS and copied it to my state assemblyperson, my state senator, and the state director of health services. The phone rang promptly the next day: someone actually speaks to me, it turns out there's the wrong number in the computer, it's all very simple.

Sometimes, when I'm holding you, nursing you, feeling the wonder of our lives together, I think: suppose this is it? Suppose you don't develop, or just develop physically; suppose you stay here, forever, unsaddled by intellect? What would be wrong with that? Suppose you just stayed in this pure animal state? Could I learn to shed those things that I have been taught that human beings should be, shed my shame, shed my disappointment, and go on loving you?

17

At two months, Max has a developmental assessment: he is functioning at the level of a three-month-old. Friends say, You must be so happy. I'm happy, but I'm not *so* happy. I know enough to know that it doesn't mean much. Still, I like to hear it: functioning at the level of a three-month-old. Once, when we were in a children's bookstore, someone said: "Five weeks old? He's so alert for five weeks!" and it made me happy for days.

Once every couple of months, we go to the regional center, part of the state system for dealing with people with developmental disabilities. Neatly dressed women who are physical therapists and nurses and social workers kneel on yellow, red and blue mats on the floor. They give Max puzzles to do; hide a plastic rabbit under a cup. "Where's the bunny? Where'd the bunny go, Max?" Through the window, I see a four- or five-year-old kid in an oversize stroller, a boy of maybe fourteen with c.p., wearing a helmet to protect his head if he has a seizure.

I say to one of the social workers: "Sometimes I worry that he'll be developing normally and then it'll just stop," expecting to hear that dismissed as a crazy fear.

"That could happen," she says.

It could?

These are the words that I'm scared of: scatter,

spasticity, low tone, high tone, flaccid, lag, c.p., seizure.

Scatter. Refers to uneven development in the brain, one faculty moving ahead while others lag behind, a sign of brain damage. Spasticity is a noun, referring to muscle tone characterized by spasm. From it, we get the word, "spastic," frequently abbreviated by junior high school kids to "spas" or "spaz," and used as a term of contempt, especially to refer to someone who is awkward or clumsy.

Seizures, formerly called fits, are electrical storms in the brain.

Because there aren't any books written about meconium aspiration babies, I read books about premies. One has a section called "The Special Child." (My friend Barbara, who is also disabled, and I used to joke that we had been "euphemized children.") It says that the symptoms of c.p. in infants can be changeable. Early on, babies might exhibit rigidity and exaggerated reflexes, but these might subside and the child would appear to be normal. But the decline in muscle tone could continue until the baby becomes floppy, unable to crawl or walk. Or it might not.

There is the fact of Max's brisk reflexes, and that his tone is somewhat low. Harvey tells us that his brain is healing.

Harvey keeps saying, "He looks very good, but it's still too early to tell."

And then, at one routine neurological appointment, we are told that Max has "mild spastic diplegia," a form of cerebral palsy.

"What does that mean," I ask, "in terms of the future?"

"I always hate having to answer questions like that," the neurologist says, "because kids always prove me wrong. But my guess would be that he'll never be a member of the Joffrey Ballet."

She advises us to get him a "jolly jumper," to have him start using a walker in a month or two.

We leave her office numb. In the lobby of the medical building, I find a pay phone and call a baby store, to see if they have a jolly jumper in stock, go right over and buy it.

It is only a few days later that I get a call from a disabled English woman who is visiting the States, wanting to meet some other disability rights activists. We make arrangements to meet: "Two, but it might be closer to two-thirty... the 10 Freeway is the Santa Monica Freeway... "

"What's your disability?" I ask.

"I'm a spastic," she says, with refreshing English forthrightness, and I feel as if someone has just handed me a cold glass of water on a hot, thirsty day.

A few weeks later, Max has another developmental assessment. The therapist who does this developmental assessment tells us the exact opposite of what the neurologist said. She says not to put him in a walker or jumper, that those would only increase his tone and cause abnormal development. But she sees none of the evidence of spasticity that the doctor had seen.

I remember a study I had seen cited in Ivan Illich's *Medical Nemesis*. In 1934, during the heyday of tonsillectomies, a survey was conducted of one thousand children from the New York Public School system. Sixty-one percent had already had their tonsils removed. The remaining thirty-nine percent were examined: forty-five percent of them were judged to need tonsillectomies. The children who were judged to *not* need tonsillectomies were examined by another group of physicians: this group of physicians found that forty-six percent needed to have their tonsils removed. The remaining children were examined by yet another group of physicians: again, nearly half were found to need tonsillectomies. Illich noted that this test was conducted at a free clinic, so financial considerations could not explain what happened. Illich cited this as an example of the fact that the structure of Western medicine pushes towards diagnosis.

I wonder how much this is true for Max – that having been defined at birth as a child with problems, doctors will now look for – and therefore find – problems. I wonder too if I'm not just engaged in some intellectually adept form of denial.

I am explaining to my friend Susan, who has lived in Nicaragua, what has been explained to us: how important it is that babies crawl, if they don't, they won't develop normally.

She laughs and says, "But, Anne, babies only crawl where there are floors. In Nicaragua, the babies don't crawl. Because the floors are all dirt floors. They get carried around on their older sister's hips until they can walk."

In April, 1986, when Max is seven months old, I go to New York, to speak on a panel and do a reading before a group of disabled women. Harilyn, the psychotherapist who leads the disabled women's group, gives me a ride to the airport afterwards.

I'm asking Harilyn how her c.p. was diagnosed. We're on the expressway. I distinctly remember that as I asked her we were going into a tunnel, but I wonder if that is right.

When her mother was giving birth to her, Harilyn says, she was ready to push before the doctor arrived, and to keep her from giving birth without the presence of a doctor, the nurses held her mother's legs together.

Harilyn says that when she hadn't walked by the age of

two her mother knew something was wrong. But one doctor said there's nothing wrong with her and another one said she had a hole in her head.

Really, a hole in your head?

Yes, really, a hole, and that I ought to be institutionalized.

God, I think, not until she was two, and her disability affects her whole body, and her speech. And guilt too: here she is, telling me about her life, and I'm feeling dread; I'm asking these questions, trying to sound neutral and friendly, while inside my heart is pulsing out its steady beat: "I don't want anything to be wrong with him. I don't want my child to be like you. I want my life to be easy."

Max wheezes with his first cold, and wheezes more with his next cold and soon has full-blown asthma. We are in and out of emergency rooms; and in my fuzzy, tired voice I am repeating again and again for tired doctors at one or two in the morning, tired doctors in stained white coats with stethoscopes slung around their necks: "He was in the ICU when he was born. He had meconium aspiration... He has a heart condition. SVT. He takes dioxin ..." Over and over again, we're told that it's a potential problem, that the medications used for asthma make the heart speed up, that's a concern with his heart condition.

Night after night, we sit up holding him so that he can breathe. Or at four in the morning Mark gets dressed and takes him out in the car; the motion of the car is the only thing that can help him sleep. I can hardly remember this, it's hazy and it didn't seem like a real crisis at the time, after all, it wasn't life threatening. It was only more hospitals, more loss of sleep, more fear of the doctors and the respiratory therapists. Why is it that respiratory therapy seems to attract such a disproportionate number of swaggering, unsympathetic men? I think most of them were pit bulls in their previous lives.

Max has pulled up his shirt so often to let doctors and nurses listen to his heart that it's one of the first words he says. When we're driving in the car, listening to the radio, and he hears it in a song, "My heart is breaking, baby," or "In my heart... " he calls out "heart! heart!" excitedly, as if they were singing the song just for him.

The night I learn my first book is going to be published, he is wheezing, and we have to leave the celebration dinner our friends have made us, and then call and say, "We're at the doctor's office now," and again, "We're still at the doctor's office," then, "We're at the hospital now." And finally, "Go ahead, eat without us, we'll do it some other time, we're just going to get take-out."

Saturday night in the hospital emergency room. Through the curtain I hear the voice of a woman who is giving her medical history: she was beaten so badly by her parents as a child that she had internal injuries. She shows the nurse her chip from Narcotics Anonymous: she's been clean for three years.

"Are you allergic to any drugs?"

"Aspirin," she says. "Well, I'm not supposed to take it. I'm taking AZT."

"HIV," one of the nurses whispers to another, and nods her head in the woman's direction.

"They're bringing in a sixteen-year-old girl," Mark says. "She shot herself. In the heart." And then we hear her moaning, the most frightening and deepest sounds I have ever heard, a cry from the heart, a cliché made real.

When we leave, we walk past a man in the corridor, a cop on either side of him, in a bright maroon pair of underpants and nothing else, his body covered with slashes from a razor blade. Did he do that to himself, I wonder? Or did someone do it to him? I don't want to have to deal with this, any of this.

*

A journal entry:

July 26, 1986. I think this is the anniversary of some revolution, although I can't remember which one. Nicaragua, Cuba?

On Wednesday, I called Laura. I dial her home number: there's a recording saying it's been disconnected. Try it again, in case I dialed wrong. Again, the recording. No, she can't have left already, without seeing me one last time. I called her at the birth center. She's living at her mother's to save on rent and to free Tay up so that he can go on up to Moro Bay. We make arrangements to get together. I hang up the phone feeling almost unbearably sad.

The next day, I learn from Tandy that Nina's baby has died *in utero*. I must have sensed Laura's sadness about that. Nina had gone to see Vi, and the baby's heartbeat was very high. She had to go into the hospital. They gave her a drug to try and bring it down, but the baby had congestive heart failure and died.

I remember how I used to sit at my desk and see Stan and Nina walk by on their way to Windward Farms or the beach – how they always looked so happy. Seeing Nina this time last year when Laura was away from the birth center having given birth to Julia and Nina was helping out: how she talked about her plans to get married; then how happy she was to get pregnant.

Robin and I come home from the group and we walk over to see the number on Nina's house so Robin can send her a note. A night or two later, I dream that I am with Nina, she is smiling, saying, "Oh, it isn't so bad. It'll just mean that I'll be pregnant for eighteen months instead of nine months."

Last night, I went to the party at Louise's for John and Sherry's wedding. We have set up a babysitting coop through the mothers' group, and Peggy and Mike took care of Max.

Before Max was born, inside, I always felt like I was seventeen years old. I remember saying to Laura, "I always knew some day I would feel like an adult." I remember too standing in the phone booth, calling Harvey at five-thirty in the morning when Max's heart alarm went off, and how I could feel each one of my thirty-three years.

At the party, for the first time since Max's birth, I feel like I am seventeen again. For a few moments I don't see the strands of grey in my friends' hair. People are dancing to Martha and the Vandellas, Smokey Robinson and the Miracles. It is 1969. We are dancing, and the future is ours. Black Panther Mark Hampton has not yet been shot in his bed by the Chicago police, Nixon has not invaded Cambodia, and we have never heard the words "Pol Pot" or "AIDS." I am seventeen years old again and I want to stay out all night.

When we get home, the only parking space is in front of Nina's house. The lights are on. Then as we are walking from there to our front door, I see Stan drive by. Stan always looked like such a kid, an unrepentant hippie. I look at his face and now he looks so old; he has the same expression that Mark and I had that long awful weekend.

Then this morning I saw Nina. We went out to the car, me and Mark and Max and her door was open. She came out. Vi was coming down the street.

"Oh, Nina," I said, and put my arms around her, both of us crying. I feel the hardness of her pregnant belly against me.

"Did you just hear?" she asks me.

"I heard a few days ago. How are you doing?" I ask, and kiss her hand.

"As well as can be expected."

Mark hugs her.

"So are you just waiting to go into labor?"

"That's what's killing Stan, this waiting."

Vi appears, in her Sunday clothes. She has just come from church. "How are you?" she says to me. "You've lost so much weight."

"When I think," Nina says, "of all the babies that I've helped come into this world, and it just happened, they just were born."

"There's a miracle baby," Vi says, bending next to Max's stroller.

"I was baking you a loaf of bread," I say, "but I ran out of butter."

"Do you want to borrow some?"

"Actually, I have to go to a Coop board meeting now."

"The food coop?"

"Yeah."

We say our goodbyes and she and Vi go into the house for coffee.

A few minutes after six that night, Lauren and I are leaving at six-fifteen to go to a Writers Union dinner, I take the loaf of bread over to Nina. I think just of leaving it on her doorstep, but the door is open and Nina says, "Come in, come in. Stay for a few minutes."

We hold hands. She says, "What's that on your hand?"

"I went to a poetry reading, and they stamped our hands when we paid. I don't know what it's supposed to be."

When they stamped it on my hand, I thought, it looks like a heart, it looks like a fetus.

"Like they do at dances," Nina says.

"I don't know why they did it at a poetry reading. It's not like people are going to leave to get high and want to come back in."

She introduces me to her parents, she tells me she is weeping sometimes but she is really doing OK. I tell her that I am one of these people who think that whole wheat bread will cure anything.

"Like chicken soup," her mother says.

"Like chicken soup," I say.

I tell her that Robin sends her love, that we heard from Tandy, we're both in one of her mothers' groups. "You know, if you could tell as many people as possible, I would really consider that a gift."

"I will. I've wanted to tell everybody in the neighborhood – so that no one will come up to you and stroke your dead belly, so that no one will say, 'When are you due?'"

Then Max is a year old and he doesn't walk and then thirteen months and then fourteen months. He's developing normally, they tell me. He cruises, holding on to things. There were late walkers in my family, my mother and my sister Jane didn't walk till they were eighteen months old.

"I'm not worried about him," one of the physical therapists says. "Walking holding on to things is walking, neurologically."

I don't care. I want him to walk, and I'm convinced that there's something wrong.

Part of getting over it is knowing that you will never get over it. One Friday, we want to go out, but we don't have a sitter. We decide to go to the drive-in.

"Would you rather see *Friday the Thirteenth, Part VI* or *Top Gun?*"

"I'd rather stay home and stare at the wall," I say.

"*Heartburn*'s showing."

I had read Nora Ephron's book from which the film was made while I was pregnant, but I'd forgotten that the main character has a crash C-section. We are sitting there at the drive-in with Max asleep in the back, and suddenly on the screen the doctor is holding up the strip from the fetal monitor and they are rushing Meryl Streep down the white halls and putting a mask over her face.

Mark and I reach out for each other.

"Oh, God," I say. "I forgot about this."

There is a moment, just before you go under general anesthesia, when you can feel the coldness of artificial sleep spreading out from the center of you and hitting your skin so that it prickles. I watch Meryl Streep going under and I am back, lying on the operating room table, and feeling that strange collision of the cold drugs against my warm skin.

I am driving to UCLA Cardiology Clinic with Max, coming down Main Street. I live at the beach, the place where rich people with views of the Pacific live and where the homeless people, who just kept moving on and moving on, end up. Cars ahead of me are braking and pulling into the left lane. I crane my neck to see what the problem is.

A man is lying face down in the street. His clothes are army green khakis, blackened with dirt; his hair is dark and matted.

I stop my car just in front of him, leave the front door open so I can hear Max. The man isn't just lying in the street, he's having a seizure, each spasm beating his face against the pavement, and it comes up bloodier each time.

I rush to the fruit store. "Please," I say to a woman who works there, "call an ambulance."

"Is he drunk?" the woman asks.

"No, he's having a seizure."

"Hmm?"

"A seizure," I shout, "call an ambulance." I look straight at her: "Call an ambulance."

I feel sick, I don't want to touch him, I don't want—one time in London, I saw someone having a seizure on the street, and another woman stopped and cradled the strange old man's head in her lap. I feel sick, I start to retch, looking at his bloody and raw face, I hate these people in their BMWs and Volvos pulling around him. I hate myself for not being able to do more.

What can I do? Am I strong enough to lift him? I can't leave Max. I hope that woman did call the ambulance. Other people start to gather. It's true, once one person stops, other people stop.

That could be my son in twenty, twenty-five years.

18

I look back over Max's "Baby's First Year" calendar:

Under a picture of a nurse in a Chinese hospital with rows of bundled newborns lying in straight rows, we have written, "September, 1985" and then:

7th: Max due. Drove on bumpy roads. Read *Spiritual Midwifery*.

13th: Contractions! Jane and Lisa fly down. Contractions stop.

14th: Wimmin's spiritual circle attempts unsuccessfully to induce labor.

15th: Drive up mountain.

16th: Spicy food.

17th: Castor oil. Lisa flies home.

18th: Contractions start.

19th: Hard labor. Max born by crash C-section at Santa Monica Hospital.

21st: Max still in critical condition.

22nd: Harvey tells us Max will live.

23rd: Anne home from hospital. Last dose of Pavulon given.

24th: Max moves finger a little tiny bit.

25th: Max opens eyes.

October. Under a picture filled with yellow sunshine, a wicker baby carriage, a terra cotta vase with pussy willows in it.

2nd: Max comes home!

3rd: Max goes to Beverly Hills.

13th: Max at UCLA Med Center. Supraventricular tachycardia.

14th: Max comes home!

16th: Mostly he lies around and looks cute.

Nov. 12th: Woman in post office says, "He looks just like a cabbage patch doll."

December 10th: Max goes to first meeting (reproductive rights).

December 19th: Max goes to second meeting (reproductive rights, again).

January 8th: Sleeps through night.

January 17th: Laughs a lot: when his monitor is put on when we lift him up and down. Max gets first cold. Daddy holds him in his arms all night long.

January 20th: First Martin Luther King Day. Max shuts down South African consulate.

January 26th: Max rolls over from front to back. Mom has a dream that he is climbing up couch.

February 8th: Max picks up coffee cup and brings it to his lips—our Java Baby!

13th: Plays with his toes a lot.

14th: Mom and Dad have fight over Max during their Valentine dinner at restaurant. Max gets lots of Valentines and tries to eat them.

15th: Apnea alarm goes off on freeway. Mom almost has a heart attack.

Under a picture of four English prams lined up outside a snack bar.

March 1st: We go out to movie. When we come home, babysitter is watching Christian rock videos and painting her toe nails bright red.

5th: Max says babababababa all the time.

20th: Max goes to Women in the Law Conference with Mom and he smiles at everyone, even Catherine MacKinnon.

24th: Max sits up and plays with his toes; Harvey tells us "the gods of good fortune have smiled" on us. Max goes off apnea monitor.

April 4th: Dr. Cokely says Max has mild spastic diplegia.

8th: Max says dadadadadada and mumumumumum-um.

15th: Blows bubbles when he talks. Teething and has a cold. Parents consider adoption.

21st: Max scoots all over house.

May Day. General strike in South Africa. Max gets first tooth.

May 24th: Takes shit in Mom's lap in Little Italy restaurant.

June 4th: So dramatic when he takes a shit!

23rd: Starts sleeping through the night.

28th: Stops sleeping through the night.

29th: Fourth tooth; leads Tykes for Dykes contingent at Lesbian and Gay Freedom Day Parade.

30th: Cries so hard he throws up. Mom is really freaked.

July 1st: We love this baby so much we just can't believe it.

There were other milestones too: the first time — months after Max was born — I went a whole day without crying. The first time I went out without leaving a note for Mark telling him where we were, so he wouldn't think we had been rushed to the hospital. The day I realized that it had been months since I had stopped obsessively checking the developmental charts in the back of the baby books. The time I let myself remember Harvey's words: "And then there are some kids who thumb their noses at the medical profession," without hearing an answering voice echoing in my head, "But don't count on it."

*

This story has a happy ending. Max is "all right." That's what people say to me, "He's all right, he's just fine," meaning, he's not at all disabled. I say, "He doesn't have any residual effects" or "None of the problems they predicted." It's important to me, to say it that way. I don't want the implication that if he were disabled, he wouldn't be all right. Or that the fact that he's not disabled means that we have no problems.

Max is almost four years old now. He can sing the theme from *Mister Roger's Neighborhood*, and do a puzzle with fifty-six pieces, say, "I'm angry." (How old was I before I could say that? Thirty, I think.) He plays his own version of baseball, calling out "You missed," if I pitch the ball to him and his bat doesn't connect with it.

It's over and it's not over.

What did I learn from it all? That nothing fits together neatly. There are no easy lessons, no clean morals. It's all random collisions, love sitting side by side with fear. It's knowing the things you already knew in a deeper way; coming to doubt the things you knew with such certainty; the surprise of learning from an infant, from someone who knows almost nothing – nothing in the sense that you are used to knowing.

How did the experience of Max's birth change me? It didn't change me at all and it changed me in every way. I still believe all the things I've believed all along about the rights of disabled infants, about women's control of our own bodies, about what illness can teach us; only now I understand the issues in a way I never could have before.

I understand now what parents face. I remember sitting in the NICU and thinking: do I want him to live; do I want him to die? Remember how I flickered off and on, off and on, all through that long, long weekend. Let him live, please let him live, no matter what. And then, a minute later: I just want this to be over. I don't care how it ends. I can't live through one more minute of this.

I think back to Dr. Holtzmann, standing above me as I lay on the gurney, saying, "Your child has brain damage." What would that have conjured up for most people? A nothing kept alive by machines. A lolling idiot, drooling, banging its head against the wall? I was lucky I could think, not just of specific diagnoses, but of people I knew and cared for with those disabilities. I was lucky to know so much more than most people know: and still I had so many fears.

I'm glad that I couldn't look into the future and see what was coming: the C-section, the near-death, the ICU, the possibility of brain damage. If I had known, I would never have had a child, and I'm so glad that I did. It's not just that I didn't know the strength I had; it's more that I couldn't have imagined how much happiness I would get out of being a mother.

I understand too, the drawbacks of taking control of your own body.

When I was pregnant, I told a friend's boyfriend that I was having a home birth.

"You're crazy," he said.

"Statistically speaking," I said (I really did use that phrase, though it seems odd and stiff now that I write it), "home births are safer than hospital births."

"I know," he said. "You're still crazy."

Months after it happened, Mark tells me that the day after Max was born, a relative called and said: "I can't believe Anne did that to her baby."

Of course, no one ever said to Lily after her son had meconium aspiration, "Well, that's what you get for having a hospital birth."

It's true, when you take control of your body, of your

birth, you take control of everything: the pain along with the joy, the bad with the good. I understand why people want to surrender their lives to someone else's power, to the power of the machine. Having surrendered, you may feel hollow inside, blank, an automaton being acted on by forces beyond your control, but at least you don't feel this awful sense of responsibility.

I understand it. But I'm glad too that I didn't succumb to it. In the end, I don't regret the decision that I made. That's not to say that if I could have looked into the future, seen what was coming, I would not have done things differently. Of course, I would have. But just as I couldn't see into the future, I can't see what the pitfalls would have been of a decision that I didn't make: who knows what might have gone wrong if I'd had a traditional, hospital birth. Knowing the self I knew in an unmedicated, wild birth – that animal self, beyond reason, common, elemental – taught me a truth I could not have learned in any other way, a truth my body had to teach me.

When I was pregnant, I used to get so sick of people saying, "You won't care if it's a boy or a girl as long as it's healthy," so sick of the assumption that health was all that mattered, that I sometimes used to say, "I don't care if it's healthy or not, as long as it's a girl." It's not a joke I would make again. Health, physical well-being does matter. It's my own internalized oppression that makes me fear having a disabled child, but it's not just that. It's the knowledge that being non-disabled is easier than being disabled. More so in this society than in others, but not just in this society. In any world I can imagine.

But to admit that disability and illness are hard doesn't mean that they are wholly negative experiences, meaningless. I had a child because I wanted something perfect to come out of me. I got just the opposite of what I thought I wanted. I don't believe in God, or any version of God, any hand of fate or karma that was out to teach me a lesson. But my child's potential disability did teach me that I don't own my child, he's not an extension of me, not there to reflect me, not there to heal my past.

Epilogue

When Max is almost two years old, I dream that I am climbing up a long flight of grey stairs that rises outdoors. I cannot see where the stairs lead. Max is next to me. We are climbing the stairs, going up and up and up; I have never climbed so far before. Up and up and up and up.

We are in the open. There is no railing. Max is beside me. This is dangerous. Up and up and further up.

And then, Max, you were falling, arms spread, legs spread, down. You didn't tumble, you fell straight and true towards earth. I turned my head away. I couldn't bear to watch.

When I knew that it was safe to look, that you had landed and were lying dead on the ground, I looked back, but you were still falling through space.

I looked away, for a long, long time, and didn't let myself look back until I was sure it was over. But you were still falling, falling for earth.

I kept turning away and waiting, waiting, waiting, not looking back until I was sure, dead sure, it was all over. And when I looked back you were always still falling.

Finally, I looked back, and you weren't falling anymore. An ocean had appeared underneath us suddenly. The waves had caught you and you were tottering out of the water, laughing, your arms raised above your head, laughing.